Animals of the Masai Mara

Adam Scott Kennedy
Vicki Kennedy

PRINCETON

press.princeton.edu

Published by Princeton University Press,
41 William Street, Princeton, New Jersey 08540
In the United Kingdom: Princeton University Press, 6 Oxford Street,
Woodstock, Oxfordshire OX20 1TW
nathist.press.princeton.edu

British Library Cataloging-in-Publication Data is available

Library of Congress Control Number 2012942088
ISBN 978-0-691-15601-9

Production and design by **WILD**Guides Ltd., Old Basing, Hampshire UK.
Printed in Singapore

10 9 8 7 6 5 4 3 2 1

Dedication

Dedicated to the wise and beautiful females of our pride

Mothers Patricia Beard and Julia Kennedy,
and Grandmothers Lillian Ollis and Patricia Saunders

For their never-ending belief and love

Contents

Mammals

Reptiles

About this book

The Masai Mara National Reserve is world famous for the Great Wildebeest Migration that passes through each year, when vast numbers of these impressive beasts march on through the daily rigours of life. However, the Mara has so much more to offer the visitor than just Wildebeest, their menacing predators and the prospect of a kill. It is an incredibly beautiful area, diverse in habitats with a high number of species to entertain and observe. These range from the classic 'Big Five' species to smaller and more elusive mammals and reptiles that will delight visitors year round, time and time again. Watching wildlife can be as easy or as in-depth as you choose to make it. But one thing is for sure, knowing what you're looking at and what behaviours to look out for can significantly enhance your safari experience.

One of the great things about mammals and reptiles is that we learn about them from a very young age; many of our first picture books taught us that E is for Elephant and Z is for Zebra, so we've all got a head start when it comes to identifying animals. Most of us are enthralled by a multitude of wonderful TV documentaries that teach us even more about our favourite creatures and inspire us to travel across continents to observe them. Many visitors to the Masai Mara arrive fully armed with a 'hit-list' of species they really must see, often having spent days undertaking the necessary homework before fulfilling their wildest animal dreams. And rightly so because safaris don't come cheap and getting the necessary time off work can take years of preparation. Maximizing your time and money should be a concern. Sometimes, however, this enthusiasm goes a little awry. You might be surprised at the number of people expecting to see a Tiger in the Masai Mara (we're sorry to burst your bubble if that includes you). And you really have to hear our Polar Bear story first-hand to believe it! But, on the whole, most visitors arrive properly prepared for 'Big Five' encounters and a whole lot more.

To help you maximize *your* Mara safari experience, this photographic guide sets out with three major aims:

- to help you identify any species that you're not sure about (you know it's a mongoose but which one?);
- to offer you lots of interesting and easily digestible information on each species; and
- to prove to you that there is so much more to look out for than just the 'Big Five'.

We want you to feel inspired by this book, to look beyond the usual and discover the unusual. We want you to have the confidence to make the right call on any animal you see. Don't just sit back and wait for your safari guide to tell you everything; pick up this book and tell them what you've just discovered – it makes for a greatly enriching experience.

If you're taking lunch at your camp or lodge and see a colourful lizard performing yoga before your very eyes, this book will not only tell you what it is, but also what it's doing and why!

Ultimately, we hope you find this field guide as useful as it is intended to be and enjoy it as much as we have enjoyed producing it.

SAFARI NJEMA!
(Good Safari!)

How to use this book

There are numerous mammal and reptile guide books available, some of which we highly recommend (see *References page 148*). From our own experiences of guiding guests in the Mara and other wildlife-rich locations, most books suffer from some common drawbacks that lend themselves to becoming user-unfriendly, especially for the novice safari-goer. These typically include over-complex and baffling text, images so small that you need a magnifying glass to see what they are, or the coverage of species being so wide that many are not found in the region that you're taking a safari.

For this reason, we have adopted a simple approach to the illustrative plates in this book, combining large, clear images with an informative, but not exhaustive, text. Most importantly, though, this information relates only to the animals that are found within the Masai Mara and its neighbouring conservancies (privately managed conservation areas – see *page 16*). We hope you enjoy the layout of this book and would warmly welcome any feedback. It's worth pointing out here that we have decided not to include one large family of mammals within this guide – the bats. Although we love bats and their fascinating behaviours, we feel that getting a good view is difficult at the best of times and making a successful identification very challenging indeed.

The classification of species is an arbitrary business conducted by very scholarly people who change their collective minds from time to time, as shown in a recent decision to rename Africa's quintessential trees from *Acacia* to *Vachellia*. This was a highly contentious move that upset a lot of botanically-minded people in Africa, not to mention old romantics like us. So, as you'll see, we've decided to ignore the latest thinking of these *floracrats* and have continued to use *Acacia* in the manner we're used to.

We've also chosen not to follow the strict scientific order of species followed by other texts (see *References page 148*). Instead, the animals in this guide are shown in a simple order which we hope is straightforward to use. This order is reflected in the *Contents* page at the front of this book, should you need to refer to it quickly.

Throughout the book, we've sprinkled snippets of information on the latest scientific thinking about the animals, and fascinating facts about how some of our featured animals received their names. These should keep you entertained while waiting for a dozy Lion to wake up or an indecisive herd of Wildebeest to cross a river.

To help get the best out of this book and the shorthand we've adopted to keep it concise, the table opposite gives an overview of the terms used in each species account.

Over the following pages, you'll find some information that we hope will enrich your safari experience. First is a summary of the geography of the Mara, so you can hold your

Common name	The name by which the animal is commonly known in English.
Scientific name	The name by which the animal is known scientifically, regardless of the local language. The names used follow those adopted by the International Union for Conservation of Nature (IUCN).
Swa:	The name by which the animal is commonly known in Kiswahili, the primary language of East Africa.
Maa:	The name by which the animal is commonly known in Maa, the language of the Maasai.
Length:	Two dimensions are given for most mammals, but only one for reptiles (these are in metres or centimetres and feet or inches): HB = head, body and tail length (*i.e.* total length); SH = shoulder height (*i.e.* the height of the mammal at the shoulder).
Gestation:	The time spent in the womb from conception to delivery.
Recognition:	A simple and concise description of the animal to aid identification.
Habits:	A synopsis of the animal's behaviour including when it is active and what it does.
Where to find:	An indication of the habitats in which the species is likely to occur.
Feeds on:	The animal's diet.

Please note: These information boxes are tinted darker (*i.e.* this colour) for species that are primarily nocturnal.

own when talking about the landscape and habitats. The next feature outlines some of our favourite places to watch wildlife in the Mara and the species you can expect to find there. Among the features we are most proud to include within this guide are the top tips and comments from a selection of the very finest safari guides working in the Mara today – and it gives us great pleasure to introduce our 'Fabulous Four' (see *page 22*).

Finally, to help keep a record of the animals you see in the Mara, a small tick-box has been included next to each species description. However, if you'd prefer not to 'spoil' your book, a checklist of the animals covered can be downloaded from the **WILD***Guides* website www.wildguides.co.uk.

Geography of the Masai Mara

The Masai Mara is the northern continuation of the Mara-Serengeti ecosystem of northern Tanzania, which covers approximately 25,000 km² (9,600 square miles). The Masai Mara National Reserve covers 1,510 km² (580 square miles), while the privately managed conservation trusts (or Conservancies) surrounding it increase the area of protected land by more than five times. It is situated in the heart of the East Africa Rift, a vast landform stretching from Malawi and Mozambique in the south to the Red Sea in the north. Within the Mara, the most obvious feature of the rift is the Oloololo-Serian Escarpment that can be seen rising in the west from most of the area. The highest elevations here reach almost 2,200 m (7,100 ft) above sea level, while the lowest parts of the Mara sit at around 1,500 m (4,900 ft). This is much higher than most people assume and helps to maintain a far cooler climate than one might expect so close to the equator. For the animals migrating here from the lower and hotter Serengeti, it must certainly feel like a winter holiday by comparison.

The bedrock of the area is incredibly old with a mix of Pre-Cambrian metamorphic rocks and younger Tertiary and Quaternary volcanic outcrops, including an attractive array of quartz-filled granites. The Oloololo Escarpment and numerous rocky outcrops are charaterized by impressive scree slopes that harbour many specially-adapted plant and animal species. Elsewhere, the soils are typically sandy in the dry north and east where expanses of *Acacia* species, especially the Whistling Thorn (*Acacia drepanolobium*) abound. In the south, soils that have been colonized extensively by grassland and savanna species show a much higher content of sodium- and potassium-rich clay, a relict residue from ancient eruptions from neighbouring volcanoes such as *Ol Donyo Lengai* in northern Tanzania.

As is typical for their respective soil types, sandy areas are well drained and retain very little surface water, while the clay-rich black cotton soils hold more moisture. Not only

Looking west across the Mara Triangle towards the Oloolo-Serian escarpment.

does this result in some permanent swamps, such as Musiara Marsh, surviving throughout the dry season, but it also means that driving conditions can be treacherous after heavy rainfall on the dark soils. Much of the excess water finds its way into one of several well-defined rivers including the Olare Orok, Talek and Sand Rivers that all meander into the mighty Mara River, which separates the National Reserve from the Mara Triangle to the west.

The Talek River.

Another important feature of the Mara is climate, especially rainfall. Although this differs markedly every year, on average two major periods of rainfall can be expected. The 'short rains' arrive in late October and typically finish by the beginning of December. Then follows a period of mild and gently warming weather until April when the 'long rains' arrive in earnest and can deliver precipitation on most days for two months. Eventually, the cool, clear skies of the southern winter arrive, from mid-June to early October, just in time for the Great Migration and thousands of human admirers to descend upon the Mara. Throughout the year, daytime

Red Oat Grass dominates the plains and is the staple food for many herbivores.

temperatures are comfortably warm between 30°C and 35°C (86–95°F), while night time rarely drops below 8°C (46°F).

This mix of bedrock, soil type, drainage, slope and climate has created a wealth of conditions that support many different types of plants. Extensive grasslands are dominated by Red Oat Grass *Themeda triandra*, a staple for many herbivores in the Mara. It should be stressed that these grasslands are kept open (*i.e.* mostly devoid of trees) because of the actions of so many herbivores, rather than the soil conditions.

The grassland is sometimes punctuated by an occasional Desert Date *Balanites aegyptiaca*, Sausage Tree *Kigelia africana* or Candelabra Tree *Euphorbia candelabrum*, although these trees survive longer on well-drained locations. Along the river systems, dense tree cover is provided by Sycamore Fig *Ficus sycomorus*, Kenya Greenheart *Warbergia ugandensis* and Orange-leaved Croton *Croton dichogamus* and the woodland surrounding Governors' Camp in the north of the reserve shows a high density of Yellow-barked Acacia *Acacia xanthophloea*. Remnant forest patches survive in the Sabaringo Valley area and feature a number of fruiting trees including Small-fruited Teclea *Teclea nobilis*, White Raisin *Grewia bicolour* and Eleodendron *Elaeodendron buchananii*.

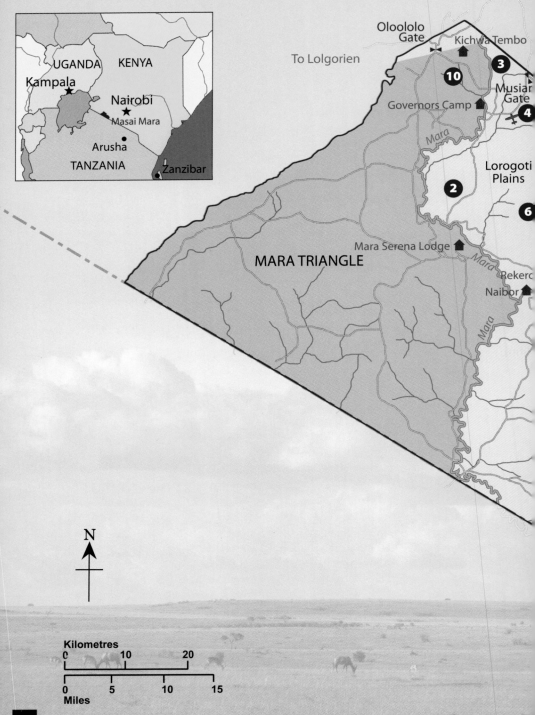

UGANDA   KENYA

Kampala

Nairobi

Masai Mara

Arusha

TANZANIA   Zanzibar

To Lolgorien

Olodolo
Gate

Kichwa Tembo

(3)

(10)

Musiar
Gate

Governors Camp

(4)

Mara

Lorogoti
Plains

(2)

(6)

MARA TRIANGLE

Mara Serena Lodge

Mara

Rekerc

Naibor

N

Kilometres
0   10   20

0   5   10   15
Miles

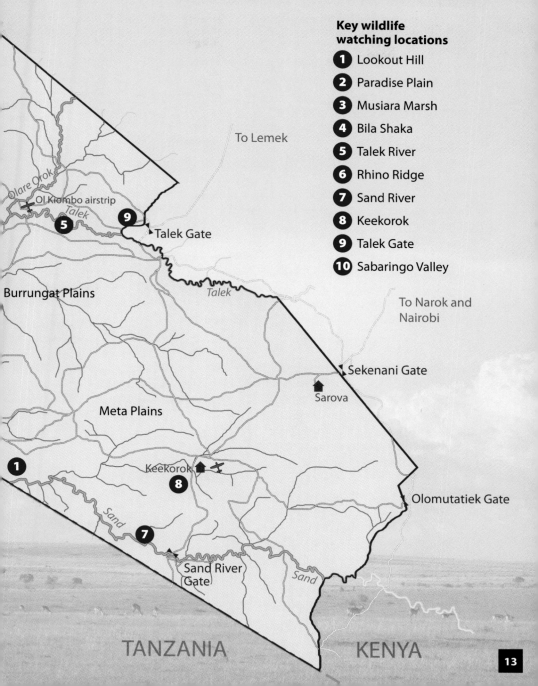

Map of the Masai Mara
showing locations mentioned in the text

Key wildlife watching locations

1. Lookout Hill
2. Paradise Plain
3. Musiara Marsh
4. Bila Shaka
5. Talek River
6. Rhino Ridge
7. Sand River
8. Keekorok
9. Talek Gate
10. Sabaringo Valley

To Lemek

Olare Orok

Ol Kiombo airstrip

Talek

5

9

Talek Gate

Burrungat Plains

Talek

To Narok and Nairobi

Sekenani Gate

Sarova

Meta Plains

Keekorok

8

1

Olomutatiek Gate

Sand

7

Sand River Gate

Sand

TANZANIA

KENYA

Where to watch wildlife in the Masai Mara

Mammals are particularly mobile creatures, especially those that migrate across national borders, but that does not mean we cannot give you a helping hand by suggesting some of the most productive areas to find them. So here are our 'Top 10' sites to search for the animals you want to see. The really good news is that even if there are few animals around, these are truly beautiful places to photograph and soak up the atmosphere. The site numbers are shown on the main map on *page 12*.

WITHIN THE NATIONAL RESERVE

1. Lookout Hill
Also known as Observation Hill, this rocky outcrop overlooks the southern stretch of the Mara River and the views from the top are nothing short of spectacular. It is one of the more reliable places to see Serval (*page 38*) and the surrounding Croton thickets are always a good place to try for Black Rhino (*page 67*) and Eland (*page 84*).

2. Paradise Plain
Featuring a vast expanse of open grassland, this is a very productive area for antelopes, especially Coke's Hartebeest (*page 102*) and Topi (*page 103*). Where small thickets occur, try searching for the secretive Caracal (*page 39*) that seeks out shade during the heat of the day. Large herds of Buffalo (*page 80*) often commute here from Musiara Marsh, and Spotted Hyena (*page 44*) can usually be seen at most times of day.

3. Musiara Marsh
Famous as the home of the Marsh Pride of Lion (*page 26*), this wetland is usually also inhabited by good numbers of Elephant (*page 62*), Bohor Reedbuck (*page 93*) and Defassa Waterbuck (*page 95*). The surrounding grassland is the most reliable area for Serval (*page 38*) sightings and you can try Yellow-barked barked Acacia woodland for Leopard (*page 30*) – although you are likely to have more luck with both cats during the cooler times of day.

4. Bila Shaka
Translating to "where there's always game", this area rarely fails to live up to its reputation and is especially good for Lion (*page 26*) and Cheetah (*page 34*) sightings. Herds of Zebra (*page 72*) and numerous antelope species are usually present and both jackal species (*pages 56–57*) are frequently encountered here.

Lookout Hill from the air.

5. Talek River

The banks of this well-wooded river are a favourite haunt of Leopard (*page 30*) and the population of Hippo (*page 68*) is quite staggering at some spots. Check the surrounding Croton thickets for pairs of Kirk's Dik-dik (*page 90*) and families of Dwarf Mongoose (*page 48*).

Keekorok.

6. Rhino Ridge

This is one of the best areas to find Cheetah (*page 34*) – so if you're in the area during the middle of the day be sure to check under the few large trees where they may be taking shade. Although this is no longer the best location to see Black Rhino (*page 67*) these days, they do sometimes occur, especially in the southern section.

7. Sand River

Some parts of the southern sector of the reserve remain undisturbed and the quiet grasslands are worth searching for Oribi (*page 89*) and Side-striped Jackal (*page 57*). As the Wildebeest migration enters the Mara from the Serengeti around this area, so do their predators including nomadic Lion (*page 26*) and Cheetah (*page 34*).

8. Keekorok and surrounding area

Keekorok is among the most established lodges in the Mara and the game here can be very approachable, making it a great place for wildlife photography. Check out the lightly wooded areas nearby for Bushbuck (*page 94*) and the rocky areas for agama lizards (*pages 140–141*).

9. Talek Gate

The short grass plains just inside the gate usually abound with gazelles, together with Spotted Hyena (*page 44*) on the look out for an easy meal. A family of Bat-eared Fox (*page 58*) can often be located with 1 km (0.5 mile) of the gate and Scrub Hare (*page 108*) are easy to find in the light scrub on both sides of the gate.

10. Sabaringo Valley

If you feel like stretching your legs, consider a walk in this attractive valley which is home to a multitude of fruiting trees that attract more primate species than any other part of the Mara. These include the Red-tailed Monkey (*page 120*). It is imperative that you take a professional guide with you in the valley as Elephants (*page 62*) are sometimes encountered along the trails. If you're staying at Kichwa Tembo/Bateleur Camp, you have the same variety of monkeys in camp without the risk of Elephants – but a walk with a guide is still recommended if you can.

THE CONSERVANCIES

At the time of writing, there are eight official Conservancies, or private conservation areas, in operation in the greater Mara area that provide a haven for wildlife and an income for the Maasai land stewards, outside of the official Masai Mara National Reserve boundary. Beyond 2012, we can expect several new Conservancies to be in operation thanks to the hardwork and determination of local communities working together with the management of the camps and lodges within them, most notably Leleshwa Camp and Siana Springs (Siana Conservancy) and Cottar's 1920s Camp (Olderkesi Conservancy). One of the major benefits of staying in most of these conservancies is the option of a night-drive – an experience that will bring a whole new dimension to your safari. If this is important to you, check for night-driving options before you book your visit.

Mara Triangle
The epitome of what a conservancy should stand for, the Triangle is superbly managed and a great place for game-drives, with the 'Big Five' regularly recorded here. There is good access to the lower slopes of the escarpment where Klipspringer (*page 91*) can be seen.

Naboisho Conservancy
The latest addition to the list of conservancies, Naboisho will soon be challenging the Triangle for the accolade of 'Best Conservancy'. It has superb game viewing throughout the year and has recently been host to Wild Dog (*page 59*). Other plus points include the beautiful scenery and few other vehicles.

Olare Orok Conservancy
Among the smallest of the conservancies but also one of the best, this area is a favourite for walking safaris. It is also excellent for nocturnal animals including good numbers of Lesser Galago (*page 117*), White-tailed Mongoose (*page 53*) and Springhare (*page 109*).

Mara North Conservancy
With breathtaking views of the Escarpment and the Mara River running by, this area is a great wildlife experience. Its rich short-grass plains and various *Acacia* species are popular with a multitude of herbivores, including Elephant (*page 62*), as well as Lion (*page 26*).

Ol Kinyei Conservancy
This conservancy offers fantastic night-drive opportunities during which a wide variety of nocturnal species may be seen – including Crested Porcupine (*page 113*), Aardvark (*page 61*), Aardwolf (*page 46*) and Striped Hyena (*page 47*).

Siana Conservancy (proposed)
The forests of Siana Springs are the best place to observe Guereza Colobus (*page 118*), usually at around 4pm, and the area is good for both species of genet (*page 42*) that appear to live side-by-side here.

ABOVE: Naibosho Conservancy.
BELOW: A map of the conservation areas surrounding the Masai Mara National Reserve.

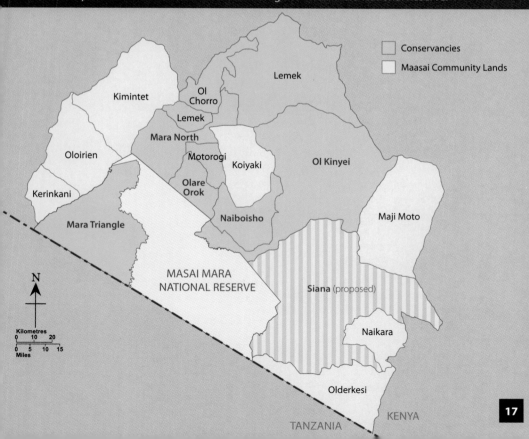

Conservancies
Maasai Community Lands

Lemek

Kimintet

Ol Chorro

Lemek

Mara North

Oloirien

Motorogi

Koiyaki

Ol Kinyei

Kerinkani

Olare Orok

Mara Triangle

Naiboisho

Maji Moto

MASAI MARA NATIONAL RESERVE

Siana (proposed)

Naikara

N

Kilometres
0 10 20

0 5 10 15
Miles

Olderkesi

TANZANIA

KENYA

The great migrations

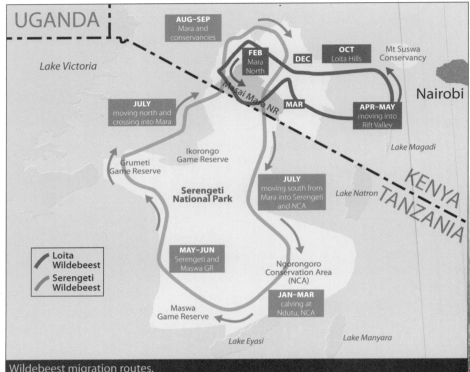

Wildebeest migration routes.

Few people are aware that the Masai Mara experiences not just one but two Wildebeest migrations each year. Most famous is the migration of Serengeti Wildebeest, which covers a distance of over 800 km (500 miles) per year, in a clockwise direction, reaching the southern Serengeti in January and beyond the northern boundary of the Masai Mara reserve in September. These are the smallest and brownest of the various Wildebeest subspecies.

The other migration is carried out by the Loita Wildebeest, which are silvery-blue in colouration, darker in tone, and around 10% larger than the Serengeti population. Their range extends from the Rift Valley in the east to the Mara in the west and they are generally found in the Mara between February and July, but this is highly dependent upon the rains.

Wildebeest crossing the treacherous Mara River.

Wildebeest migrate in search of fresh green grass and fresh water. Although grass remains in the areas they have departed, the quality of the grass is the defining factor and reason for their continued movements. The effect of grazing and the addition of dung and urine ensures that the grass will be of good quality when the herds return the following year. As scientific research techniques continue to improve, we are learning even more about the sensitivities of the herds to salt and mineral concentrations in particular. Phosphorus levels in the grass are now known to be very important to the movement of Wildebeest and biologists are striving to learn even more about how the herds are able to determine the levels of this crucial element. The current theory is that the animals do so through hyper-sensitive taste glands. Other minerals can be detrimental to the animals' health if their concentrations are too high, especially if these are in their drinking water, and it might be possible for the herds to taste dangerously high levels of certain elements and decide to move on.

A migration of a different kind

Following the Wildebeest on their migration is a fascinating species that benefits from the huge volume of dung left behind. Although the Dung Beetle is most often seen climbing over a pile of gnu poo, it is a capable flier and takes to the wing in order to keep up with its highly benevolent donors. At each stop, the beetle will roll a few dung balls and lay its eggs within, giving the emerging larvae a nutritious start in life before undergoing a metamorphosis into the winged adult beetle. There may be three generations of Dung Beetle within each annual Wildebeest migration.

The leap of faith...

Another major benefit to migration is the reduction in predation by big cats and hyenas. For the most part, these predators tend to have fixed territories, pride areas or home ranges. Although the migration will pass through these areas, Wildebeest numbers suffer less because these are fixed. This is best explained by looking at Lions, which, with the exception of nomadic individuals, are fixed to a pride area. When the migration passes through a pride area, Lions will feast for a period of 1–2 months. However, after the herds have left the Lions are dependent upon other food sources which, for the most part, also tend to move with the Wildebeest or changes in food and water availability. Consequently, the number of Lions within a pride are restricted by the amount of game found within the pride area throughout the year. If the Wildebeest were to stay in just one area, the size of the Lion pride would increase. Wildebeest therefore benefit by travelling through numerous smaller prides of Lion on a regular basis rather than staying within the territory of one large pride.

River crossings and other dangers

Animals of both sexes and all ages travel together and can cover long distances in a single day, usually at a slow, plodding pace but occasionally at a canter.

In the Mara, however, they face one major obstacle – the mighty Mara River. As with the majority of their movements, Wildebeest are motivated to cross this dangerous river by the prospect of fresh green grass on the other side. The sandy banks are very steep in many places and many animals are killed by injuries sustained when descending and ascending these obstacles. Once they reach water, the flow of the Mara River can be powerful enough to sweep animals downstream where many also perish. At numerous locations along the Mara in August and September, the river is littered with tens, even hundreds, of Wildebeest corpses that are feasted upon by Marabou Storks and various vulture species – nature's garbage-cleaners.

The river also contains some of the continent's largest Nile Crocodiles, which are ready and waiting for the herd to swim alongside their hidden jaws in the murky waters. Finally, and for those that survive these obstacles and make it to the far bank, many herds are likely to run into an ambush by Lions that will have been watching them in anticipation for hours.

Plains Zebra will often wait for Wildebeest to cross first.

About the guides

There is no doubt that your safari guide can make or break your safari experience – though having travelled extensively across East Africa for many years, we can say with some authority that the level of guiding in Kenya is up there with the very best. This is partly due to the education and training facilities provided by the Kenya Professional Safari Guide Association (KPSGA).

It has been a privilege and a pleasure to have worked closely with the guides at Naibor Camp and also to have had the opportunity to get to know so many genuinely helpful and knowledgeable guides across the Mara. It is because of our great respect for them that we've chosen to include some of their experiences and wisdom within this guide. Let's face it, they spend far more time in the field than the rest of us and they really know their stuff. So it is with great pride that we present to you our 'Fabulous Four' who have very kindly shared their thoughts, experiences and knowledge with us.

Jackson Looseyia

Jackson is familiar to many as one of the presenters on *Big Cat Live!* and *Planet Earth Live!,* and is among the most sought after guides in East Africa today. The son of a hunter-gatherer father and Maasai mother, his cultural experiences were expanded further by attending Catholic school. But as a child Jackson found his own peace in wild places by watching the birds and animals around him. He co-founded the local Koiyaki Guiding School, was influential in the creation of the Naboisho Conservancy and now runs Nomadic Encounters. His favourite animal is the Leopard because it can bring down animals twice its size: "What amazing strength to then lift them into a tree."

David Lekada Mpusia

David was born in the village of Aitong in the northern part of the Mara in 1972. He is proudly Maasai and has enjoyed watching wildlife all his life – but only turned to professional guiding in 2006. His guests appreciate his relaxed manner, steady driving and incredible eyesight and the authors can testify that David can spot a Lion more than 1 km (over half a mile) away – amazing! He is qualified to KPSGA Silver-level and currently works as a freelance guide which allows him more free time to spend with his family. He has a particular fondness for Giraffe: "They're elegant and so peaceful, I just love a Giraffe!"

Joseph ole Kima

Jospeh is another proud Maasai, born in the early 1970s in Olmesutie. With some reluctance, he was forced to attend school by the Government of the time but soon became a model student. He began working with Kichwa Tembo (&Beyond) as their in-house naturalist in the late 1990s and has been guiding professionally since 2000. Today, he is one of the very best guides in the Mara with a wealth of knowledge, fascinating stories and personal experiences. His favourite animal is also the Giraffe on account of their beauty and long eyelashes although Joseph readily admits to "being a sucker for any baby animal" too.

Petro Naurori

Born in Talek village in the heart of the Masai Mara in 1979, Petro has been guiding professionally since 2003. With a KPSGA Bronze-level certificate under his belt, he has worked as a full-time guide with several camps since then but has recently turned freelance. His favourite animal is the Cheetah: "I love the way it hunts in the open and is very selective of its prey." He also confides that he loves its speed, something that will come as no surprise to those that know Petro!

Our only regret is that limited space has not allowed many more guides to contribute their knowledge and stories here but the good news is that you'll probably be getting it first hand from some of them very soon!

Mammals

☐ **Lion** *Panthera leo*

Length: HBT 350 cm / 138" (male), 275 cm / 108" (female); SH 120 cm / 48" (male), 100 cm / 39" (female).

Gestation: 15 weeks.

Recognition: a large, sandy-coloured cat whose tail ends in a hairy tuft. Adult males are significantly larger than females and exhibit the bushy mane for which the species is famous.

Habits: typically active during the cooler hours, especially at night, and tends to spend much of the day sleeping and grooming. However, hunting during the middle of the day is not uncommon, especially when food is abundant such as during the Wildebeest migration.

Where to find: savanna and open plains, rarely forest.

Feeds on: a variety of herbivores ranging in size from hares and young gazelle to Cape Buffalo and Maasai Giraffe. In the Mara, Wildebeest and Plains Zebra are most frequently taken.

Among the most popular of all animals likely to be encountered in the Mara, the Lion is easy to identify. But it is the behaviour of this creature that is most fascinating and our understanding of it continues to increase with new studies and observations. Most importantly, this is the most sociable of all African cats, living in prides of related females (often 3–6) and their offspring that are dominated by an unrelated male, or collective of males (usually brothers or father-son groups) known as a coalition. Some prides may number as many as 40 animals but this is rare. When numbers reach a high level the pride usually breaks up, particularly when food becomes scarce within their territory, or pride area. The norm is for males to be ejected from the maternal pride when they reach 2–3 years old, which is when their manes start to become visibly bushy. Such males become nomads until they mature, when they then compete with other males for the privilege of heading their own pride. Until that point, males, and occasionally females, will roam across an area without a pride, known as a range. The main reason that all males are forced to move on is to avoid them breeding with related females.

It can be a tough life for a young male Lion but, once he has matured and taken over a pride, he can enjoy a wonderful life. He can mate with all pride females and,

With regard to Lion behaviour, the Mara could rewrite all the text books ever written about this amazing animal. Almost every day, we see behaviour that was not previously known. For example, there is one well-known male, known as Notch, who regularly goes 'on safari' with his four fully-grown sons: he defends them, they defend him and they regularly feed each other. This is totally opposite to what adult males are meant to do.

Another powerful coalition of four male Lions moved into Musiara Marsh in 2012 and took over a unit of the Marsh Pride. In the process, they ousted two older, unrelated males but when one of these animals neared the brink of death from starvation, he was allowed by the new pride males to feed with them. This is unheard of and completely staggering behaviour. The Lion's story is always being re-written. ***Jackson Looseyia***

The Lion, the 'King of the Jungle', is a keystone species, its populations reflecting the general health of the environment. To those with the power, please take care of them.

Male

although he may take the 'Lion's share' on kills, is rarely required to take part in hunting, which is the preserve of the quicker and more agile females. Males will usually dominate a pride for 3–5 years, during which time they may sire many litters of cubs and defend the pride against other males. Typically around the age of ten, and after years of sustained fighting with rival males, he may be defeated by a fitter and stronger male, or coalition of males, and toppled from the pride. This is often the end of his era as he is unlikely to find another pride to dominate. With his strength and speed diminished and being unlikely to be able to make successful kills alone, he may eventually starve.

Female Lion, or *Lioness*, are longer-lived, frequently reaching 15 years or more. They are the day-to-day hunters of the pride and will often stalk prey together, although each has her own skills and preferred place in the hunt. Once prey has been located, the Lionesses will encircle it and stalk to within 20 m or so before running at great speed and bringing the prey down. Lion lack stamina and rarely chase prey far, frequently giving up the chase once they are beaten. Their key to success is to get as close to the prey as possible without being noticed – which is probably why most hunts take place at night. Once prey has been brought down it is quickly strangled with a sustained biting grip to the throat, or a suffocating grip

over the mouth and nostrils. Due to the abundance of male coalitions in the Mara, it is quite common to encounter them on a self-made kill, often on large and dangerous species such as Hippo. Lion are not above scavenging either and take prey from other predators, given the chance.

It is most common to encounter a pride of Lion sleeping or resting under a shady tree, and these huge felines indulge in restful activities for around 20 hours a day. An important activity you may encounter is mating, which can occur at any time of year as long as females are actively fertile, or in oestrus. Bouts of mating continue for 5–8 days during which time the 'honeymoon couple' may mate 2–3 times per hour, every hour, leaving no time (or energy!) for other activities such as hunting and eating. Each mating session generally lasts for between 5–10 seconds, so if you want to photograph it you need to be ready with your camera.

Three and a half months later, a litter of 1–4 blind and heavily spotted cubs are born in a well-hidden den, away from the pride. Their eyes open after a week and, at three weeks, the cubs are mobile, curious and very playful – but in danger from predators such as Spotted Hyena, Leopard and eagles. However, the biggest threat to the new generation is from a new male Lion who has taken over the pride. Infanticide among Lion is surprisingly common and, although very disturbing, ensures that the new pride male sires his own offspring. Females losing their cubs in this way will be induced into oestrus again with a few weeks and the cycle begins for her again.

Only 25% of Lion cubs reach two years of age but those that do are showered with affection by their mothers and warmly received into the pride by other Lionesses. Social grooming takes numerous forms, including head rubbing and licking, and there are few sights as magical as a harmonious pride taking time to enjoy life and each other. Other communications include the famous "roar" which is usually given when night falls as a proclamation of territory. Males are the loudest and can be heard as far as 8 km / 5 miles away, but females also roar. Scent marking is also common, with males urinating on prominent bushes and rocks being a common sight.

Although Lion are apex predators (*i.e.* they are at the top of the food chain), their numbers have decreased significantly in Africa over the past 60 years, from an estimated 400,000 in the 1950s to just 20,000 today. Much of their former habitat has been lost to an expanding human population and agricultural development, while many thousands are still killed each year as a result of predator-livestock conflicts, including many within the Masai Mara and the surrounding conservancies.

Female or *Lioness*

Leopard *Panthera pardus*

Swa: **Chui** Maa: **Olkinya lasho**

Length: HB 275 cm / 108", SH 80 cm / 32"

Gestation: 13–14 weeks.

Recognition: a beautiful large, spotted cat with short legs, a long, white-tipped tail and robust build. Also look out for the very long, white whiskers.

Habits: mostly active at night with best sightings often in early morning and late afternoon. Stalks its prey before carrying it up a tree to devour.

Where to find: open savanna, forest and riverine woodland.

Feeds on: a variety of mammal prey from hares to large herbivores up to the size of adult Wildebeest. It is especially fond of Impala, Warthog and Olive Baboon, and also birds such as Helmeted Guineafowl.

Easily identified from the larger Lion (*page 26*) by its heavily-spotted coat and white-tipped tail, the Leopard is more likely to be confused with the slimmer, longer-legged Cheetah (*page 34*). A Leopard's spots are arranged in circles, or rosettes, creating an incredible camouflage that allows it to stalk its prey to within a few metres before pouncing on the unsuspecting victim and killing it with a stranglehold to the throat. Although adult Eland (*page 84*) and young Giraffe (*page 76*) are sometimes taken, the Leopards of the Mara rarely prey upon such large animals, possibly due to their relatively small size compared to Leopards found elsewhere. Leopard are famous for their tree-climbing ability and routinely carry prey, often heavier than themselves, in their powerful jaws up into the higher branches where it is safe to feed without

Chief Stalker
The ability of a Leopard to hide in grass while moving with stealth is second to none. Adults have been seen to walk into short grass only 40 cm / 16" high, disappear for 5 minutes and eventually emerge some 20 m / 65 ft away!

harassment from Lion and Spotted Hyena (*page 44*). These two powerful predators are the biggest dangers facing a Leopard, but Leopards are often aware of their presence and steer well clear. Despite being a favoured prey item, Olive Baboon (*page 126*) also represent a threat and troops will often force a Leopard, through noisy and aggressive intimidation, to leave an area.

Leopard are usually encountered alone, with the major exception being a mother with her cubs. Males take no part in the rearing of cubs and their mating encounters, usually with more than one female within their home range, are kept brief and highly secretive. The commonly heard vocalization of Leopard is a loud pulsating "*saw-grunt*" usually repeated up to 15 times, sounding like a carpenter sawing wood. Home ranges are routinely marked with urine and favoured trees are used as scratching posts, both offering clues to their presence.

Before giving birth, a female will hide in a dense thicket where the cubs (usually 1–4) are born and kept hidden for around 2 months. It is during this time that the cubs are most at risk from predation by wandering Spotted Hyena. The cubs will stay with the female for the next two years, sometimes less for male cubs, and it is not unusual for two generations of cubs to be encountered together with their mother.

Although it is the most widespread of all African cats, the Leopard is also among the least known especially when it comes to their social and family behaviour. Often considered to be solitary animals, truly sociable, almost pride-like, behaviours are increasingly being observed in the Leopards of the Mara.
On several occasions I have witnessed a grandmother, mother and cubs from two litters hanging out and even hunting together. Maybe this behaviour hasn't been recorded elsewhere because Leopards are usually very shy – so who knows whether this is normal or not?
Jackson Looseyia

This Bohor Reedbuck, weighing almost twice that of the Leopard, was hauled up this tree for safety.

Cheetah *Acinonyx jubatus*

Swa: **Duma**   Maa: **Olowuru kerri**

Length: HBT 240 cm / 95"; SH 85 cm / 34"

Gestation: 13–13½ weeks.

Recognition: a large, long-legged and streamlined cat with a small head. Its sandy-coloured head, coat and tail base are heavily spotted, though its underparts are white. The face has prominent black 'tear-lines' running down from the eyes. The long tail has 4–6 bands towards the end and a white tip.

Habits: mostly active in the daytime, when it searches for prey, but males frequently patrol their territory at night.

Where to find: open plains and savanna.

Feeds on: mostly Thomson's Gazelle and hares, although larger prey to the size of Wildebeest, Topi and Zebra are sometimes taken when several animals hunt together.

Although superficially similar to the Leopard (*page 30*), the Cheetah has a truly spotted coat and is far more slender, like a greyhound in structure. It has a well-deserved reputation for being the fastest land animal on the planet, reaching speeds in excess of 112 kph / 70 mph, including an impressive 0–100 kph / 0–60 mph burst in three seconds, when chasing prey. Otherwise, the Cheetah is the lightweight of the 'big cats'. Its delicate frame makes it highly susceptible to damage from scavengers and predators, such as Lion (*page 26*) and Spotted Hyena (*page 44*). They are particularly at risk from these more powerful predators when sitting over a kill and will often give up their prey rather than face a potentially damaging encounter.

Cheetah detect their prey by sight, which is exceptionally acute. The black 'tear-mark' running down from the corner of the eyes

What's in a name?
The Cheetah is the only feline with non-retractable claws and its scientific genus *Acinonyx* translates to 'no-move claw' in Ancient Greek.

helps to keep sunlight from obscuring their vision. Sometimes this cat will climb onto a high termite mound, or even a vehicle, for an elevated view of the terrain. Once prey has been located, it is stalked to less than 30 m / 100 ft before being chased over a distance of up to 500 m / ⅓ mile. During this time, the large nostrils swell to allow increased air intake and the respiratory system works overtime to circulate oxygen through the body. The long tail is used for steering and balance, especially when chasing the fleet-footed Thomson's Gazelle (*page 100*) that habitually twists and turns during a chase. At the final moment, the prey is usually tripped before being pounced on and a fatal choke-hold applied to the windpipe. Because the heart is racing so fast, the Cheetah has to allow its body to recuperate before eating, often for as long as 25 minutes. Once it has cooled down it will gorge itself before circling vultures give away its position to dangerous scavengers. Females live and hunt alone within a home range after reaching maturity at around 2 years old, while males mature earlier at around 1 year. Males may live and hunt in a coalition and their territory includes the ranges of several females. Both sexes are promiscuous and each litter may include offspring from several males. Most litters are of 3–6 cubs, which are born with their characteristic spots and downy, grey fur which they eventually shed. A high percentage of young cubs are killed by

A mother with her well-grown cub.

predators but once they reach about 6 months they are generally safe and able to follow their mother on hunts. However, they are not particularly skilled until 15 months or so. At 18 months, the mother leaves the cubs, which then stay together for another 6 months, refining their hunting and social skills. When they are about 2 years old, the females of the family desert their siblings to lead a solitary life.

One of the biggest problems facing Cheetah is their low genetic variability, which causes problems with health. In fact, all Cheetah surviving today are the result of an inbreeding event, known as a genetic bottleneck, that is likely to have occurred between 10,000 and 12,000 years ago. The latest DNA research suggests that as few as 7 Cheetah survived at one point, all of which were descended from the same female.

Unlike other big cats, Cheetah purr but cannot roar. They also produce a loud bird-like "chirp" when trying to find each other and may hiss loudly in the face of danger.

Because the territories or home ranges of Cheetah are so huge, it can be very difficult to pin-point where to find them, especially as they sometimes move at night. I have watched a Cheetah on the Burrangat Plains just before sunset and seen the exact same animal outside of the reserve the following morning. They prefer shorter grass in which to hunt and have a fondness for safari vehicles, sometimes jumping onto them to benefit from a higher viewpoint to spot the next meal and also to look out for threats. **David Lekada Mpusia**

An energetic youngster takes a break from play.

☐ **Serval** *Leptailurus serval*

Swa: **Mondo** Maa: **Eseperua**

Length: HBT 130 cm / 51"; SH 60 cm / 24"	
Gestation: 9½–11 weeks.	
Recognition: a small, spotted and blotched cat with disproportionately long legs and neck, short tail and large ears.	
Habits: shy, solitary and mostly nocturnal but sometimes encountered in daytime as it hides in long grass, and very rarely with kittens.	
Where to find: open grassland, lightly wooded savanna and open marshes, including Musiara.	
Feeds on: hares, rodents and birds, but sometimes reptiles and amphibians.	

The Serval is a quiet and stealthy hunter that uses its large ears to locate prey in long grass. It frequently pauses to listen for the sound of movement, using its acute sense of hearing to locate its prey before leaping with an enormous pounce. Once caught, the prey may be played with before being swallowed whole. Like the Caracal, this cat is also capable of impressive vertical leaps of 3 m / 10 ft or more, swatting birds clean from the air. These animals prefer to hide from danger, including game-vehicles, and usually press themselves close to the ground to avoid detection. When threatened, particularly by larger cats, they will arch their back and hiss loudly. Solitary males mark their territories, which usually contain more than one female, by spraying urine onto bushes, while females tend to be accompanied by 1–4 kittens that are well hidden, often in a burrow, long grass or a bushy den.

Given a partially hidden view, look out for the black backs to their ears which show a crisp white spot in the middle.

These two cats may not have the same appeal as their three larger cousins but anyone fortunate enough to encounter either should consider themselves extremely lucky!

Caracal *Caracal caracal*

Length:	HBT 120 cm / 47"; SH 45 cm / 18"
Gestation:	9–11 weeks.
Recognition:	larger than a domestic cat and more athletic in build with a tan coat and delicate black ear tufts.
Habits:	solitary and mostly nocturnal but occasionally seen by day.
Where to find:	grassy plains with thickets, wooded savanna and rocky hillsides.
Feeds on:	birds and mammals up to the size of Impala (*page 96*).

Often called the African Lynx on account of its long-tufted ears, the Caracal is not a lynx at all but a relative of the forest-dwelling Golden Cat *Caracal aurata* of central Africa. Similar in size to the Serval, the coat is tan-red with whitish underparts in adults, while kittens tend to be lightly spotted on their bellies. Despite its size, the Caracal is a formidable hunter that has been known to tackle adult Impala and very large birds, killing them by strangulation. Meetings between rival males can be violent, especially when a female in oestrus is present. Although females may be followed by a male for days, it has been known for them to mate with several males during a single period of oestrus. The litter of 1–3 kittens is typically well hidden but once they are 4 weeks old the mother will move them almost daily as she travels in search of food.

What's in a name?
The English and scientific name Caracal derives from the Turkish word *karakulak* meaning 'black ear'.

Caracals are often accused of stealing small goats and lambs but they can also hunt much larger prey. They are very strong and have that feline ability to jump on the back of prey and simply hang on until the prey tires and can be easily brought down by piercing the veins in its neck or closing off its windpipe. ***Jackson Looseyia***

Wild Cat *Felis sylvestris*

Length: HB 120 cm / 47"; SH 40 cm / 16"	
Gestation: 9 weeks.	
Recognition: almost identical to its descendent, the domestic cat.	
Habits: solitary, very shy and primarily nocturnal.	
Where to find: rocky outcrops, savanna and dry acacia scrub but nowhere common.	
Feeds on: birds, lizards and small mammals, especially rodents and hares.	

Among the most secretive of all animals to be found in the Mara, the Wild Cat is notoriously difficult to find and any encounter with it must be considered very fortunate indeed. Domestic cats are likely to be encountered close to villages and hybridisation with the Wild Cat's human-friendly cousins represents the biggest threat to its survival as a pure wild species. A Wild Cat is generally taller and in better condition than a domestic cat and typically shows a lightly striped coat and warm reddish tones behind the ears.

Male cats are quite vocal when attracting mates and pairs come together in season but soon separate. Females rear the litter of up to five kittens alone, usually in an underground den but sometimes among boulders and dense vegetation. Not surprisingly, the Wild Cat "*meows*" and "*purrs*" just like a domestic cat.

Length: HBT 140 cm / 55"; SH 40 cm / 16"	
Gestation: 11 weeks.	
Recognition: half-way between a cat and a dog in appearance with a heavily striped and blotched coat, banded tail and a distinctive racoon-like face.	
Habits: a solitary and nocturnal prowler.	
Where to find: well-wooded areas, acacia scrub and savanna, often near water.	
Feeds on: just about anything from plant matter and invertebrates to small mammals, reptiles, birds and their eggs (*i.e.* omnivorous).	

A close relative of the genets (*page 42*), the African Civet is taller and stockier but, similarly, most likely to be encountered around sunset or at night when it wanders widely in search of a varied menu. Small mammals, such as mice, are leaped upon and seized in the powerful jaws before being thrashed from side to side.

Among the Civet's other impressive attributes is an erectile crest that it raises when threatened, excited or alarmed. During the breeding season, males will serenade potential mates with a laughing "*hahaha*" call. In the daytime, this animal will rest in dense vegetation but only the females make a nest in which up to four pups are reared.

Does this make scents to you?
African Civets mark their territory with a highly pungent scent secreted from the perineal glands at their rear. Unfortunately for the Civet, it was discovered 100s of years ago that this yellow waxy secretion, known as *civetone*, has the ability to fix the scent of flowers in the production of perfumes. Consequently, civets were kept in huge numbers around the world, generally in poor conditions. Thanks to progressive action by animal welfare groups, such as the World Society for the Protection of Animals (WSPA), this cruel practice has all but stopped, with major perfume manufacturers adopting a synthetic substitute since the 1990s.

Small-spotted Genet *Genetta genetta*

Swa: **Fungo** Maa: **Eshiminsa**

Also known as Common Genet

Length: HBT 100 cm / 39"

Gestation: 10–11 weeks.

Recognition: off-white coat colour shows linear black spots, a black stripe down the spine, and an evenly-barred tail usually tipped with white.

Habits: nocturnal and can become tame around camps and lodges.

Where to find: prefers drier habitats and is more frequently seen on the ground than the Large-spotted Genet.

Feeds on: an omnivorous diet of fruits, birds, invertebrates, small mammals and reptiles.

Genet Generalities

Genets are long-tailed, short-legged *viverrids*, a family that also includes the African Civet (*page 41*). Unlike that terrestrial species, both genets featured here are mainly tree-dwellers that climb superbly but also venture to the ground to feed and scent-mark. Like the African Civet, these cat-like mammals have fragrant scent glands at their rear and often make impressive handstands while rubbing the glands against a tree or bush. Generally solitary, genets may gather together where a substantial food source permits non-aggressive behaviour between them. Their diet consists mostly of small rodents but the extent to which they feed on birds, small reptiles and invertebrates depends on local availability. Prey is typically leapt upon before being despatched with a killer bite to the neck.

The leafy nest is usually in a tree-hole where 1–5 kittens are raised. The young do not accompany their mother on hunts until they are several months old and are usually chased away when they are mature at six months. Most activity occurs from one hour before sunset until the early hours of the morning and your best chance of seeing one is at your camp or lodge where many become habituated to night-time feeding stations. This is when you are most likely to hear their cat-like vocalizations and smell their not-so-pleasant scent!

Large-spotted Genet *Genetta tigrina*

Swa: **Kanu** Maa: **Esiminsha**

Also known as Blotched Genet

Length: HBT 110 cm / 43"

Gestation: 10–11 weeks.

Recognition: a large, warm-toned genet with irregular rusty blotches and an unevenly barred tail, usually topped and tipped with black.

Habits: nocturnal and can become tame around camps and lodges.

Where to find: forest and mixed woodland; more commonly seen in trees than the Small-spotted Genet.

Feeds on: an omnivorous diet of fruits, birds, invertebrates, small mammals and reptiles.

Small-spotted Genet ▲

Large-spotted Genet ▼

43

Length: HBT 200 cm / 79"; SH 90 cm / 35"

Gestation: 16–17 weeks.

Recognition: a large, spotted, muscular predator with a sloping back and large, round ears.

Habits: gregarious and primarily nocturnal, hyena enjoy bathing in pools to keep cool.

Where to find: savanna, sometimes open grassland and marshes.

Feeds on: large insects to big game; an effective hunter and scavenger.

The Spotted Hyena suffers from seriously bad public relations and we feel a strong obligation to put the record straight on this formidable hunter and wonderful parent. Often content to scavenge on just about any carcass it encounters, the Spotted Hyena is also a superb athlete capable of chasing and catching a wide variety of game, especially Wildebeest (*page 104*) and Plains Zebra (*page 72*), but also larger prey including Cape Buffalo (*page 80*). Most prey is run down by small groups of Hyena that may chase for 6 km / 4 miles or more before wearing out the exhausted animal, which is unceremoniously eaten alive! Where Topi (*page 103*) are numerous, such as on the Burrungat Plains of the southern Mara, Spotted Hyena patrol through dozing herds until an unsuspecting victim is quickly taken. Amazingly, a single Hyena can devour a Thomson's Gazelle fawn (*page 100*) within 5 minutes and a large pack of hungry Hyena will consume a whole adult Zebra within an hour, bones, teeth, hooves, EVERYTHING! Specialized teeth and incredibly powerful jaws make light work of the largest animal bones from where the highly nutritious marrow is extracted. Strong gastric juices enables digestion of such bony materials within 24 hours, resulting in chalk-white faeces. At the carcass, vultures are tolerated because of the symbiotic relationship they share; Hyena will often follow descending flocks of vulture to a carcass. Their biggest threat comes from Lion (*page 26*) but a pack of Hyena will often prevail unless an adult male Lion is present.

Spotted Hyena society is female-dominated and highly complex in comparison to other carnivores. Females are noticeably larger than males and the alpha-female, or matriarch, rules the clan, which can number over 50 individuals. Rather bizarrely, a female's genitals are almost identical in size and proportion to a male's and the sexes are best separated in the field by the presence of nipples on the female. Courtship and mating occurs throughout the year and can be amusing to watch as males fear females intensely and the act can be a rather delicate procedure. Two dark-brown, bear-like cubs are born in a communal den that is usually taken over from an Aardvark (*page 61*) or Warthog (*page 70*).

These cubs are the largest of any carnivore in relation to the mother's size and are born with their eyes open. The larger of the two tends to bully their weaker sibling and may eventually kill it. Alpha-female offspring inherit dominance over other females but the males will leave the home clan in search of another once mature. Although the alpha-male gets the privilege of mating with more females. he is not permitted to take part in rearing his own offspring.

Who's laughing now? Hyena communication is primarily vocal and the characteristic "*whooo-woop*" is among the most familiar sounds of the African night and is used as a rallying call. Other calls of note include the giggling cackle and the classic laugh, which is used at the carcass to express excitement and sometimes danger. They also whimper, grunt and growl.

Length: HBT 110 cm / 43"; SH 45 cm / 18"
Gestation: 14 weeks.
Recognition: similar to Striped Hyena but less hairy and much smaller, about the size of a jackal (*page 56*). Its pointed ears are pink and its legs and muzzle are slender.
Habits: nocturnal and often solitary, but can be sociable.
Where to find: dry acacia scrub and less frequently on grassy savanna where termite mounds are plentiful.
Feeds on: almost exclusively harvester termites (up to 200,000 per night!), rarely other invertebrates and their larvae.

Although a close relative and similar in appearance to hyenas, the Aardwolf is the sole species in its own subfamily, due to its diet and physiology. Unlike the hyenas, which have a diet of bone and flesh, this mini-hyena is a termite-eating specialist, retrieving thousands of the ant-like insects at each sitting using its long, sticky tongue, very much like a Pangolin (*page 60*) or Aardvark (*page 61*). It has five toes on its front feet, like the *viverrids* (the African Civet (*page 41*) and the genets (*page 42*)), rather than four as in other hyena, and its rear teeth (molars) are relatively fine compared to those of its bigger, bone-breaking cousins. Although preferring to seek out termite mounds alone, they typically live in loose colonies and will move dens every few months in order to seek out new feeding grounds and allow favoured termite colonies to build up in numbers again. Pairs are monogamous and share parental duties. They use their anal glands to lay pungent scent trails – their faeces smell strongly of ammonia, due to the thousands of soldier termites they consume.

Length: HBT 160 cm/63"; SH 75 cm/30"	
Gestation: 13 weeks.	
Recognition: smaller than Spotted Hyena (*page 44*) with a bushier tail, shaggier mane and longer, greyish coat with dark stripes running vertically from the spine to the legs. The ears are darker than those of the smaller Aardwolf and are long and pointed compared to the stout, round ears of the Spotted Hyena.	
Habits: strictly nocturnal; mostly solitary.	
Where to find: dry acacia scrub with open areas.	
Feeds on: mostly a scavenged diet of carrion but also invertebrates, reptiles and small mammals.	

mostly on bones at partially devoured carcasses, but also preys on invertebrates and rodents. Striped Hyena are less sociable than Spotted Hyena but breeding pairs are family-oriented, with both sexes involved in caring for the striped pups. Their dens are frequently self-dug although some are gentrified burrows of Aardvark (*page 61*). Den sites can usually be identified by the abundance of bones littering the site. This species is significantly less vocal than Spotted Hyena and their subtle chattering "laugh" is unlikely to be heard. Instead, it maintains contact using pungent scent glands at the rear which, like the African Civet (*page 41*) and genets (*page 42*), it smears onto vegetation as markers.

Rarely encountered, apart from in the dry acacia zone, these nocturnal creatures leave their dens after dark and return well before sunrise. The diet consists of less fresh meat than the Spotted Hyena; it rarely hunts large mammals, preferring to scavenge

Fearless and sometimes aggressive, these animals are very much feared by the Maasai because they are more likely to attack people than Spotted Hyena. They are mainly nocturnal and are very bold in their behaviour.   ***Jackson Looseyia***

☐ Dwarf Mongoose *Helogale parvula*

Length: HBT 35 cm / 14"

Gestation: 5–6 weeks.

Recognition: the smallest mongoose, with a rusty-brown coat and tail.

Habits: diurnal, terrestrial and gregarious, with family groups usually numbering 10–25.

Where to find: savanna and riverine woodland with numerous termite mounds.

Feeds on: invertebrates and small reptiles.

At first glance, this mini-mongoose could be mistaken for a reddish squirrel but is in fact the smallest carnivore in East Africa. It is highly vocal and will alert its clan to danger with a high-pitched, muffled whistle "*pissoo*" before running at speed into cover. When it is relaxed, you may also hear a gentle piped whistle, while angry confrontations between individuals are usually punctuated with low growls.

This is a highly sociable mongoose and lives in extended family units ruled by a dominant pair, usually the oldest, which have sole mating rights. Other members of the clan will assist in bringing up the litter of pups and subordinate females may also suckle them. All males are ejected from the clan as they reach maturity and join a new clan. Young females usually stay with the clan and await their turn for dominance before gaining breeding rights. This species is only active in the daytime and sleeps in groups, for safety and warmth, within termite mounds and hollow fallen trees.

Banded Mongoose *Mungos mungo* Swa: **Nkuchiro miraba** Maa: **Ekisherin sampin**

Length: HBT 70 cm / 28"

Gestation: 9 weeks.

Recognition: a grey-brown mongoose with heavily grizzled fur, long tail and 10–12 obvious dark bands across the back. Appears hunch-backed when running.

Habits: diurnal, terrestrial and gregarious, with family groups usually numbering 15–40.

Where to find: grassland and open savanna.

Feeds on: primarily invertebrates but also enjoys birds' eggs and small reptiles.

By far the most abundant and frequently seen species of mongoose in the Mara, the Banded Mongoose is frequently encountered in extended family units, led by a dominant female. While some members of the clan search for food, most of which is dug up from the ground, others will stand erect on lookout duty and alert others to danger with alarm calls specific to threats from land or the air. The biggest threats come from the air, the most dangerous being the Martial Eagle – although it has been known for groups of this mongoose to mob the predator and force it to drop a captured clan member. Twittering calls and grunts are used to maintain contact as the group searches widely for prey during early morning and late afternoon, avoiding the heat of the midday sun. Large and toxic prey items may be rolled around, while eggs and hard-shelled beetles are repeatedly thrown backwards against a rock to crack them or to make access easier.

An entire clan will den together, often in a termite mound or disused burrow with multiple entrances to aid ventilation and access. Outsiders are not tolerated and pitched battles occur at territorial boundaries with fatalities quite common. Within the clan, social grooming takes place frequently and is used to build bonds between individuals. The most aggressive behaviour occurs during female oestrus when numerous males squabble for mating rights. Otherwise, Banded Mongoose life is harmonious, with all members of the clan involved in raising the pups.

Slender Mongoose *Herpestes sanguineus*

Length: HBT 65 cm / 26"

Gestation: 9 weeks.

Recognition: notably slender with short legs, grey-brown coat and a long, black-tipped tail that is almost as long as the body.

Habits: diurnal, rarely strays far from cover and, although usually encountered at ground level, is adept at climbing trees.

Where to find: forest edge, well-wooded savanna and marshes.

Feeds on: just about anything it can find, including fruits and seeds, invertebrates and small vertebrates, including venomous snakes.

This small but very aggressive mongoose, is the only one feared by birds, which frequently raise the alarm in their presence. It is fond of birds and their eggs and frequently climbs trees to find its quarry, using specially adapted claws and foot pads. Unlike the larger but otherwise similar Ichneumon Mongoose that drags its tail behind it, this species carries its tail high off the ground when walking or running. It is most likely to be encountered in well-wooded areas. Like the Dwarf Mongoose (*page 48*) the Slender Mongoose exhibits variable coat colouration according to the climate and soil-type of the area in which it is found; in the Mara it tends to be a cold, greyish-brown. Male Slender Mongoose are polygamous and frequently share a home range with several females.

☐ Ichneumon Mongoose *Herpestes ichneumon*

Swa: **Nguchiro mkubwa**
Maa: **Ekisherini**

Length: HBT 110 cm / 43"

Gestation: 10 weeks.

Recognition: large and otter-like, with a grizzled grey coat, long black-tipped tail, short black legs and a dark face.

Habits: diurnal and often encountered in pairs or family groups (up to seven).

Where to find: short grasslands, open savanna and the dry acacia zone but rarely far from water and dense scrub.

Feeds on: invertebrates, fruits and eggs but most fond of small vertebrates, especially large snakes including Spitting Cobra (*page 142*).

This is the longest of all mongoose and is always on the move. It trots with an obvious 'slinking' action that is not dissimilar to an otter, always with its nose low to the ground and tail trailing behind, sometimes with the black tip raised. It is a good digger and swimmer and takes a wide variety of prey items including fish. Males typically have several females within their home range, each of which gives birth to 2–4 young that may travel together like a train, each joining up to the one in front and always led by the mother.

What's in a name?
The English and scientific name *Ichneumon* (pronounced "*ik-new-mon*") derives from the Ancient Greek for '*tracker*', the famed enemy of the dragon in historical literature.

Marsh Mongoose *Atilax paludinosus*

Also known as Water Mongoose

Length: HBT 100 cm / 39"

Gestation: 9 weeks.

Recognition: a bushy-haired, all-dark mongoose with a thick, tapering tail.

Habits: mostly nocturnal but also active during the cooler hours of day when it may be seen swimming with head raised clear of the water.

Where to find: lives close to water and marshes.

Feeds on: aquatic invertebrates, small vertebrates and sometimes fruits.

This is the most dextrous of all mongoose and handles food items, such as crabs and clams, with the agility of a primate, and will frequently use rocks to break open tough objects. The soft and sensitive padding on the paws helps the animal when searching for prey underwater. In the daytime, it may be encountered following well-used pathways along watercourses and, if alarmed, it may take to the water when it could be confused with an otter. Although the coat is dark, it appears to 'shine' when wet. This species has been recorded performing an unusual hunting behaviour. It may sit with its bright-pink anal glands exposed, which contrast against the dark coat, while emitting squeaking calls. These calls attracts small birds to investigate and once they get close the mongoose pounces on them for a quick kill.

Length: HBT 120 cm / 47"	
Gestation: 8–9 weeks.	
Recognition: a large grey mongoose with black legs and a pointed white-tipped tail.	
Habits: solitary and nocturnal, emerging before sunset to patrol grassland and scrub.	
Where to find: forest edge, wooded savanna and mixed grasslands.	
Feeds on: mostly invertebrates but also small mammals, birds, reptiles and amphibians.	

This is the largest of all mongoose species in East Africa and probably the most athletic as it searches for food throughout the night covering many kilometres at a steady trot. It shows a distinctive hump-backed appearance and rarely stands erect on its rear legs like some other mongoose species. Like the Marsh Mongoose, it possesses an impressive anal gland that produces an intoxicating fluid that is sufficiently pungent to keep predators at bay. This same fluid is also used as a territory marker and during any observation of this animal you may see it rub its rear against grass stems and small bushes, laying a trail of scent as it does so.

What's in a name?
As with the Ichneumon Mongoose (*page 51*), the scientific name of this species derives from the same Ancient Greek word *Ichneumon*, meaning 'tracker' while *albicauda* describes the 'white tail'.

■ Zorilla *Ictonyx striatus*

Also known as Striped Polecat

Length: HBT 60 cm / 24"	
Gestation: 5 weeks.	
Recognition: black shiny coat with four long, white stripes running from the head to the tail; resembling a small skunk. The long, bushy tail is whitish and usually the same length as the body.	
Habits: strictly nocturnal and solitary.	
Where to find: savanna and acacia scrub.	
Feeds on: invertebrates, small rodents and young birds.	

This slender little carnivore is the smelliest of all African animals by virtue of the horrendous scent that is produced from the anal gland. This scent causes a burning sensation in the nasal passage of other mammals. While scavenging at a particular carcass, a Zorilla was observed to keep a pride of nine Lion at bay by spraying them with scent. Zorilla is well-known among the Maasai as it shares the short grassland surrounding the Mara where sheep and goats are usually grazed. Several Maasai shepherds have testified to their dogs running away from this small, striped mammal at night but few have ever seen it in the daytime when it prefers to sleep underground, especially under the roots of an established bush. Otherwise, very little is known about this fascinating creature – the Skunk of Africa!

What's in a name?
You may notice that Zorilla and White-tailed Mongoose (*page 53*) share the same Maasai name, *Olpelis*, which means 'stinky one'!

■ Honey Badger *Mellivora capensis*

Swa: **Nyegere**   Maa: **Enkowaru oonaishi**

Length: HBT 110 cm / 43"	
Gestation: 26–28 weeks.	
Recognition: low-slung, broad and flat-bodied with black below and grey above, separated by a white border. Walks with a distinct 'waddle' and runs at a steady trot with tail raised.	
Habits: primarily nocturnal, wandering widely in search of food, often in pairs.	
Where to find: widespread where thick cover occurs but avoids flooded areas.	
Feeds on: plant matter, invertebrates, honey, large reptiles, small mammals and carrion – a true omnivore.	

Notorious for their ferocity and fearlessness in the face of danger, Honey Badgers will think little of taking on a pride of Lion (*page 26*), a pack of Spotted Hyena (*page 44*) or a Leopard (*page 30*) if challenged. When attacking people, they aim for the genitalia – so be warned!

A Honey Badger's coat is exceptionally loose-fitting, so if a predator bites into it it can easily turn around and bite back with powerful jaws and tear with its bear-like front claws. The canine teeth are surprisingly small for such a large carnivore but the rear teeth (molars) are perfectly built for crushing its varied diet. There is little doubt that this animal has a sweet tooth as it has forged a fascinating symbiotic relationship with a bird, the Greater Honeyguide, in order to find beehives and honey. Once the bird has located an active hive, it will find a Honey Badger, call to it and then lead it to the honey pot. The badger uses its claws to rip open the hive and the two species share the spoils. It has been rumoured that bees become 'suffocated' by the pungent scent of the badger, released from its anal glands, and thus steer well clear! Either way, the Maasai people prefer to hang their beehives from trees to keep Honey Badgers away.

Black-backed Jackal *Canis mesomelas*

Also known as Silver-backed Jackal

Length: HBT 135 cm / 53"; SH 38 cm / 15"

Gestation: 9 weeks.

Recognition: fox-like with a black-and-silver saddle and a black-tipped tail.

Habits: most active at night and cooler periods, sheltering in cover during the daytime heat.

Where to find: common across savanna with mixed grasslands and scrub.

Feeds on: just about anything from invertebrates to large snakes, medium-sized mammals and birds. Also a calculating scavenger at the carcass.

This opportunist is best separated from the Side-striped Jackal by its black-tipped tail. Despite its smaller size and lighter frame, the Black-blacked is the more proficient hunter, tackling live prey up to the size of Impala (*page 96*), bringing the animal down after a chase with bites to the leg, loin and throat. At the carcass, it annoys larger predators, such as Lion (*page 26*) and Spotted Hyena (*page 44*), with one Jackal distracting while another jumps in to steal a morsel. Black-backed Jackal are much noisier than Side-striped, making high-pitched yelps in communication with its pack, especially at night and when food has been located.

Side-striped Jackal *Canis adustus*

Length: HBT 125 cm / 49"; SH 40 cm / 16"

Gestation: 8–10 weeks.

Recognition: slightly larger than Black-backed Jackal with a clearly defined white stripe running along the flanks between the front and rear legs. The tail is more bushy than in Black-backed and shows a white tip.

Habits: most active at night and cooler parts of the day, sheltering in cover during the daytime heat.

Where to find: wooded savanna and open plains, though rarely seen.

Feeds on: an omnivorous diet but less predatory than Black-backed Jackal.

This scarce resident of the Mara is rarely encountered but is almost certainly overlooked. The white stripe on each flank, usually edged in black, is the best identification feature – but also look out for the white-tipped, bushy tail and smaller ears. This species is less willing to chase adult antelope than Black-backed Jackal but will seek out newborns hidden in the grass. It is also less vocal than Black-backed Jackal, often calling a mere "*hoot*" and a stuttered series of yaps.

Day of the Jackal

The social unit of both jackals consists of a monogamous pair that mates for life and discourages outsiders by marking the territory with urine and faeces. They den in a disused burrow where each pair typically rears 2–6 pups. Births generally coincide with a glut of food; in the Mara this is when the Wildebeest (*page 104*) migration arrives and when antelope calve. Pups become more playful as they mature and although most young leave the territory after one year, some will stay on as 'helpers' to their parents.

Bat-eared Fox *Otocyon megalotis*

Swa: **Bweha masigio** Maa: **Esiro**

Length: HBT 100 cm / 39"; SH 35 cm / 14"

Gestation: 9–10 weeks.

Recognition: shows a grizzled grey-brown coat with black legs and a short pointed muzzle, above which sits a black eye mask and huge ears.

Habits: mostly nocturnal and sleeps for much of the day, emerging from burrows in the cooler hours to forage. Runs for cover when threatened.

Where to find: short-grass plains.

Feeds on: invertebrates, especially termites but also small mammals, birds and their eggs.

Those fantastically large ears are designed for locating prey, down to 30 cm / 12" below ground, which it digs up with scurried paws. Combined with an acute sense of smell, very little gets past this tenacious little carnivore. Its jaws contain up to 52 teeth, the most of any African carnivore, which are much smaller, relative to body size, than any other canine and are used for crushing its prey. These attractive little foxes enjoy a leisurely life on the plains, often spending hours outside the den just waiting for the air to cool before heading out on hunting missions. It is not uncommon to see them rifling through Zebra and antelope dung, picking out juicy beetles. It is believed that pairs mate for life and raise up to six pups per litter in a disused Aardvark or Warthog burrow. This underground den is core to their range but they dive down one of many other 'escape dens' if harassed by a predator or vehicle.

☐ **Wild Dog** *Lycaon pictus*

Length: HBT 153 cm / 60"; SH 75 cm / 30"

Gestation: 10 weeks.

Recognition: a lean, long-legged dog with a blotched coat of black, tan and white, huge ears and a bushy, white-tipped tail.

Habits: sociable, most often seen at rest or trotting in pack formation.

Where to find: savanna, acacia scrub and woodland, but very rare.

Feeds on: small to large antelope, from Kirk's Dik-Dik to Greater Kudu.

The Wild Dog is the most successful hunter of all large carnivores, with 85% of all hunts resulting in a kill compared to just 30% for Lions. They hunt in packs and spook herds to identify the weakest individual and then run it down (they have a top speed of 64 kph / 40 mph). The victim is gradually weakened before members of the pack grab a limb and the animal is ripped apart. Larger prey items are generally brought down by one Wild Dog grabbing the tail and another the face, while others disembowel the animal. These are otherwise gentle and sociable canines with an admirable social make-up. The pack is controlled by an *alpha* pair, which has the right to breed and scent-mark their range. All other pack members assist in hunting and ensuring the well-being of the litter, which usually consists of 5–12 pups. All females leave the pack after 2 years and join other packs. Males stay with the pack in which they were born. Injured or older dogs often stay behind with the pups but all are given a healthy share of the kills through regurgitation. Submission and non-aggression are the norm with these dogs and it is thought that this helps to maintain a healthy pack. The range of a pack can extend beyond 2,000 km^2 and animals seen in the Mara are likely to visit the Serengeti during their annual movements. Once common in the Mara, the Wild Dog was exterminated following an outbreak of canine distemper but signs of a comeback are looking positive. They are, however, declining elsewhere in Africa due to persecution by farmers who kill them over livestock losses.

What's in a name? The scientific name derives from the Ancient Greek for 'wolf' *lycaon* and the Latin for 'painted' *pictus*.

Pangolin *Smutsia temminckii*

Swa: **Kakakuona** Maa: **Entaboi**

Also known as Ground Pangolin or Scaly Anteater

Length: HBT 111 cm / 44"

Gestation: 19 weeks.

Recognition: has a tiny head and a long body and tail uniquely covered in large plate-like scales.

Habits: Primarily nocturnal but occasionally seen during the day curled up in a tight ball.

Where to find: could be found almost anywhere except in marshes and rivers, but very rare.

Feeds on: ants and termites (*i.e.* it is formicivorous).

This enigmatic creature is high on the wish-list of even the most experienced safari-goer, such is its rarity. The armour of hard scales, made of keratin (just like your fingernails), covers all but the head and underbelly, which it protects by rolling into a tight ball when threatened or sleeping. If harassed by a predator, it will thrash its tail, using the sharp scales to cut like blades. The front claws are long and curved and used for digging into termite mounds and anthills. However, these are cumbersome to walk on, so the animal generally walks only on its hind legs, with the tail used as a counterbalance, and with forelegs raised. It extracts its tiny prey using the very long tongue (50 cm / 16") that is loaded with sticky saliva and stored in a cheek pouch. Once common, Pangolin has been systematically poached across its range for its scales, which are in demand as love charms and by witch-doctors.

The Maasai name *Entaboi* means "impossible to believe it exists" and I shall always remember the date I saw my first and ONLY Pangolin (4th September 2005). As I stopped my vehicle nearby, it curled into a defensive ball and I remembered my grandfather's advice to me about this creature. I made a large circle with twigs around the animal leaving 18 gaps – the number of gaps you are able to leave in the circle before the Pangolin leaves predicts the number of houses within my future *boma* (village unit). This meant lots of cows, wives and children. I was very happy that day! **Joseph Ole Kima**

On average, most Elephants spend 16 hours a day eating approximately 200 kg / 440 lbs of plant material, although in excess of twice that amount has been recorded! Their digestive system is relatively simple and inefficient. As a consequence, their dung consists mostly of nutrient-rich plant fibres and is often colonized by fungi. The remainder of the day is spent on the move, relaxing and sleeping.

Conservationists often struggle to protect Elephants from farmers and villagers whose crops are destroyed by their actions – but pioneering research into the reaction of Elephants to honey bees may hold the solution to this conflict (see elephantsandbees.com *page 148*).

Together with the Wildebeest (*page 104*), Elephants are crucial to the maintenance of the Mara ecosystem, as they consume vast numbers of young trees that would otherwise turn the open plains into a wooded savanna.

During the wetter months, Elephants are easily found around Musiara Marsh as they like the long grass there. During the drier months (July to November), that coincide with the Great Migration, most of our Elephants head north of the Mara, as they dislike the noise and chaos that comes with so many Wildebeest. Instead, they spend several months creating havoc in the local villages.

David Lekada Mpusia

Breast-feeding taking place between a mother's front legs.

The Horn of Africa

Rhino horns are not attached to the skull and are made from keratin, the same protein substance that forms human hair and fingernails. Unfortunately, both Black and White Rhinos are in serious danger of extinction due to demand for their horns from Chinese and Vietnamese pharmacists, who claim the horn has medicinal qualities for fever, rather than an aphrodisiac as is usually claimed. This follows on from the Middle-Eastern craze, during the latter half of the last century, of using Black Rhino horn for dagger handles, which caused the population to crash from 70,000 in the 1950s to fewer than 2,500 by 2004. If the high levels of poaching continue, these spectacular mammals may soon disappear completely – so enjoy them while you still can.

Black Rhinoceros *Diceros bicornis*

Length: HBT 4·4 m / 14 ft; SH 1·8 m / 6 ft

Gestation: 65–70 weeks.

Recognition: a huge mammal with a barrel-like physique, short, thick legs and two horns along the top of its head.

Habits: generally reclusive and nocturnal but occasionally bold and shows well in the cooler parts of the day.

Where to find: prefers wooded savanna and woodland, but most likely to be encountered on grassy plains.

Feeds on: a carefully browsed diet of leaves, branches and shoots. Even when feeding in open grassland, it selects herbaceous plants and micro-shrubs rather than grass.

Often the most difficult of the 'Big Five' to see in the Mara, the Black Rhino is second only in weight to the Elephant (*page 62*). The naming of the two African Rhino species has been grossly corrupted since their discovery by Dutch colonists hundreds of years ago, with the White Rhino originally being given the Dutch name *wijd*, meaning 'wide', on account of its long, square-shaped upper lip. The second species was hastily called Black Rhino, no doubt because some individuals appeared much darker – but the colour of the tough skin is usually a direct result of the soil, mud or dust that the animal has rolled in, and little more. The proposed alternative names of Square-lipped (White) and Hook-lipped (Black) Rhino have not been well-received. Separation of the two species is not a problem in the Mara as White Rhino do not occur in the wild here.

The difference in lip shape is a result of the differing feeding habits; White is a grazer (*i.e.* it eats grass), while Black is a browser that uses the prehensile upper lip to pluck leaves from branches.

Their huge size and horns make them formidable in the face of adversity and they are very rarely killed by Lion (*page 26*) or Spotted Hyena (*page 44*), although very young calves are occasionally taken. Males use their horns to battle, sometimes fatally, over access to females, and the Black Rhino is reputed to have the highest rate of same-species mortal combat of any mammal. Although they have poor eyesight, both their hearing and sense of smell are very acute and it is difficult for any animal to approach them without detection. Any threat is generally met with a loud grunt or sneeze-cough before running away at speeds of up to 50 kph / 30 mph with the tail raised high. Smell is the primary sense used in communication, with adults of both sexes spraying pungent urine onto bushes and defecating in dung piles, or middens, to inform other Rhino of their presence. Like Hippo (*page 68*), male Rhino are retromingent, meaning they urinate backwards. Males are generally solitary except when females are in season, when he may follow her for up to 2 weeks, conducting routine urinalysis (see *The taste test, page 99*). Females are generally accompanied by calves that stay with her until she calves again, and sometimes long after that. Mating is a time-consuming process as males usually make several attempts to mount before success, with copulation then taking up to 30 minutes.

Hippopotamus *Hippopotamus amphibius*

Length: HBT 4·5 m / 15 ft; SH 1·6 m / 5 ft	
Gestation: 34–35 weeks.	
Recognition: a huge pink and grey-brown blubbery giant, with massive front teeth.	
Habits: usually in water during daylight hours, emerging at dusk to graze on land through the night.	
Where to find: major rivers but also seasonal pools, occasionally on land in daytime.	
Feeds on: mostly grass and rank vegetation. Occasionally nibbles on carcass meat.	

Often labelled 'the most dangerous large animal in Africa', the Hippo is often encountered relaxing in rivers and pools where they appear quite the opposite. Most human fatalities are attributed to canoeists cruising on occupied stretches of river or people accidentally coming between a Hippo and its nearest escape route to water. Despite its huge size and short legs, a Hippo will outrun any human and has been clocked at over 30 kph / 17 mph. Those massive front teeth are spear-shaped incisors and recurved canines, comprised of ivory, rather than keratin like the rear teeth (molars). They are used primarily as fighting tools in territorial disputes, often involving intimidation, charging and water-tossing before contact. Hippo are sociable creatures, living in mixed-sex pods dominated by an ill-tempered bull who presides over his stretch of the river and harem of up to 30 females. He defends this vigorously against other males that try to usurp him. Young males are tolerated within the pod for as long as they show subservience to him, usually by defecating and/or urinating in the face of the 'boss'.

This species is well adapted to a semi-aquatic life, with its eyes, ears and nostrils placed high on the head affording it good sensual perception while keeping cool in the water. Many budding naturalists are inquisitive about why these pink, naked giants do not suffer from sunburn. During periods of drought, many will suffer from dehydration and burnt skin, but under normal conditions the Hippo is able to sunbathe for about an hour per day. This is thanks to a unique red and acidic skin secretion that offers anti-bacterial and ultra-violet absorption qualities. During these sunbathing sessions, it is

What's in a name? The common and scientific name *Hippopotamus* derives from the Ancient Greek for "river horse".

common to see oxpeckers and other bird species de-lousing the Hippo of skin parasites and ticks.

Hippo will generally stay submerged for 5–6 minutes but experienced canoeists on the Zambezi River, in Zambia, claim to have witnessed dive times of up to 15 minutes. Mating takes place in the water, with males lying on top of submerged females, her nostrils occasionally making it to the surface for breath. Birthing of a single calf, rarely twins, usually takes place in the water but also on land close to water. These 30 kg / 66 lb water-babies are able to suckle underwater within minutes. All but the youngest members of the pod vocalize loudly, with numerous grunts and a "*wheeze-honk-honk-honk*" being the most familiar calls. Dominant males proclaim their territory with a painfully whining song, given on average once per month, which sounds like they have a terrible toothache! At dusk, Hippo commute from the river to their grazing grounds, shuffling along well-worn paths, known as 'hippo trails', which can wear down by several inches. On land, they are less territorial and will graze in mixed pod associations, walking up to 8 km / 5 miles in search of grass, and consuming around 40 kg / 88 lbs per night. They are occasionally observed chewing on a carcass, which should be considered a sign of nutritional stress rather than enjoying a delicacy.

Defecation usually takes place in the water during the day and is an interesting spectacle, with vigorous shaking of the paddle-like tail ensuring the muck is spread widely. On land, various members of the pod will shower territory markers, known as middens, with dung. These middens are usually lone bushes that remain well-fertilized for years. As with Black Rhino (*page 67*), Hippo are retromingent, meaning they urinate backwards.

Pig or Whale?

Great discussion surrounds the origins of the Hippo. As terrestrial even-toed ungulates of the order Artiodactyla, they are classified together with Warthog (*page 70*) and other swine. But many scientists believe they share a common ancestor with cetaceans (*i.e.* whales and dolphins).

An adolescent takes a stroll.

Warthog *Phacochoerus africanus*

Swa: **Ngiri or Pumba** Maa: **Olbitir**

Length: HBT 200 cm / 79"; SH 65 cm / 26"

Gestation: 20–26 weeks.

Recognition: a large-headed dark pig with a shaggy reddish-brown mane, obvious tusks and wart-like growths on the face.

Habits: diurnal, feeds in family groups and runs with the tail raised high – like an antenna.

Where to find: common on open plains and in savanna and forest edge.

Feeds on: grasses, rhizomes, roots and tubers, occasionally carrion.

The fabulous Warthog is a favourite among safari-goers because it has so much personality. Usually encountered in family groups, they can be tricky to photograph on the plains as they are keen to flee from danger. But in some camps, such as Kichwa Tembo, where they enjoy grazing on the lawns and dig up nutrient-rich food items, they have become very tame and approachable. Even where they appear tame, Warthogs must always be treated with respect, as those formidable tusks are razor-sharp and quite capable of slicing

What's in a name? Although the Kiswahili name for Warthog is *Ngiri*, the success of the Disney animation *The Lion King* has resulted in them being known widely as 'Pumba', after the Warthog character in that movie. This is an abbreviation of *mpumbavu*, meaning 'idiot'!

through flesh. Both sets of canine teeth protrude from the mouth; the top tusks are the longest but the lower set much sharper – so be warned! The tusks are frequently used for digging but are also used in hog-to-hog combat and defence against their numerous predators. Adult Warthog are favoured by Lion (*page 26*) and Leopard (*page 30*); the piglets frequently being taken by Cheetah (*page 34*) and sometimes birds of prey. At sight or sound of danger a fleeing Warthog will attempt to escape to a bolt-hole, reversing in at the last moment to face any threat with its tusks. This technique frequently ends happily for the Warthog and occasionally very badly for a Lion.

When feeding, Warthogs break up the soil with their pointed snouts, tusks and feet. You may see them feeding on bended knees, resting on thick-skinned, calloused pads with their front legs tucked underneath. While this is a common sight

Kneeling affords better access to short grass.

in the Mara, Warthogs do not practice this habit everywhere. Although Warthogs are very capable of digging their own holes, they frequently take over abandoned burrows of other animals, such as Aardvark (see *page 61*), and seem happy to share their den with birds, such as the Sooty Chat, which may provide early warning of approaching danger. In fact, in good company, Warthog can be very friendly indeed and will sometimes allow Banded Mongoose (*page 49*) to groom them for ticks and other parasites.

Although Warthog have a long, reddish-brown mane, they are otherwise mostly hairless. As a consequence, they have difficulty with temperature regulation, but cope with this by huddling close together on cold mornings or wallowing in mud or water during the heat of the day. Wallowing causes discolouration of the skin and as a result the animals acquire the colour of the mud, clay or sand in which they bathe.

A group of Warthog is known as a sounder and often consists of several related females, or *sows*, and their piglets. Males, or *boars*, tend to be more solitary but commonly follow females that are ready to mate. After two weeks of nursing in a birthing den, piglets will follow their mother on feeding trips. Perhaps surprisingly, hogs (swine in general), are the only hoofed animals that produce litters of multiple young – it is not uncommon to see sows with up to eight piglets in tow – although predation takes a heavy toll.

The facial 'warts' of a Warthog consist of thickened skin and are most obvious in males, which have two pairs: one below the eyes and another above the tusks. These warts appear to afford some protection in combat. The warts of females are much smaller, most animals having just one small pair below the eyes.

Plains Zebra *Equus quagga*

Swa: **Punda milia** Maa: **Oloitiko**

Length: HBT 3 m / 118"; SH 1·4 m / 55"	
Gestation: 52–56 weeks.	
Recognition: an unmistakable striped horse.	
Habits: highly sociable, mixing well with other species. Active day and night and regularly enjoys a dust-bath.	
Where to find: grassland and savanna.	
Feeds on: mostly grasses but also other plants.	

Instantly recognizable from our first alphabet books, the Zebra is a nomadic species in the Mara, with many roaming resident herds supplemented by vast numbers of Serengeti migrants between July and October. Although not as populous within the Serengeti-Mara

What's in a name?
The Kiswahili name *Punda milia* literally translates to 'striped donkey'.

ecosystem as Wildebeest (*page 104*), Zebra can appear to outnumber their more famous travelling companions at times. This is especially so during the early part of the Great Migration when they feast as pioneer grazers on the long grass, paving the way for short-grass specialists to follow. Adopting a safety-in-numbers defence strategy, Zebra are often found in mixed-species herds, although they are better equipped for survival than many other herbivores with superb eyesight and acute senses of smell and hearing. Herds huddle around their foals at the first sight or smell of danger and the dominant male, or *stallion*, is an active chaser of predators

Disputes can become boisterous.

including Lion (*page 26*) and Spotted Hyena (*page 44*). Zebra are highly manoeuvrable and are often able to outrun predators – but failing that will send a dangerous rear kick into the face of danger, occasionally making painfully loud contact. Like many other plains game, Zebra live in family units, or harems. These are dominated by a single stallion who serves up to six females, or *mares*. Multiple harems move together as herds. Zebra society is surprisingly complex, with

This highly communicative species uses vocalization, body posture and numerous ear-flagging signals to get a message across.
These are a few examples:
Neck outstretched = greeting
Ears forward = frightened
Ears erect = alert or friendly
Ears backward = angry
Snort = tense
Loud bray = danger

a distinct hierarchy between the mares and their foals, grooming being used as a method of gaining rank.

Males without a harem live in bachelor herds until they are old enough to challenge for one – often an aggressive encounter. Upon winning a harem, the stallion inherits mating rights with all the females. The brown-and-cream foal is active soon after birth, staying close to its mother for several months before bonding within the rest of the harem.

A frequently asked question is "Is the Zebra black with white stripes, or white with black stripes?" Most authorities consider them to be white with black stripes, as the white bellies are not striped. However, some evidence suggests that they are black in the womb and acquire the white stripes and belly just before birth. So, it would seem the jury is still out... Whatever the truth, it's certainly not black-and-white!

A mother and foal

Another frequently asked question is "What function do the stripes serve?" Numerous explanations have been offered over the years but some of the more credible include:

Camouflage – the Zebra's main predator, the Lion, is colour-blind and hunts mostly at night. Therefore, when it looks through long, vertical grass in search of prey, you can understand how effective this flamboyant camouflage could be.

Dazzle – when a predator chases into a herd of Zebra, it must be difficult to fix focus on an individual while being dazzled by a multitude of stripes heading in different directions. Oddly enough, the collective noun for Zebra is 'a dazzle'!

Heat Regulation – black attracts heat and white reflects it, so perhaps this theory has some merit.

Identity – each Zebra has a unique pattern of stripes, so maybe the 'bar-code' theory is true...

☐ Maasai Giraffe *Giraffa camelopardalis*

Swa: **Twiga**   Maa: **Olcharkuk**

Length: TH 5·2 m / 17 ft

Gestation: 60–62 weeks.

Recognition: unmistakable with very long legs and neck and a latticed coat.

Habits: moves slowly in loosely associated groups.

Where to find: open plains, acacia woodland and savanna.

Feeds on: deciduous foliage and twigs, shrubs and fruits by browsing but also eats grass.

Watch out for Giraffe bending down to pick-up bones, which they suck and chew on to obtain vitamins and minerals. But what really amazes me is that Giraffe have just 8 vertebrae – that's the same as you and me and all the other mammals.

David Lekada Mpusia

Giraffe gather in loose associations of females and their young. Older males tend to be solitary, while younger males gather in bachelor groups. Giraffe are collectively known as a 'tower' when standing, or a 'journey' when on the move. Sexing Giraffe is easy, even when the 'undercarriage' is not in view. Males shows flattened, bald-topped horns, while females and young show hairy-tufted horns. These horns, or ossicones, are fused to the skull (unlike antelope) and males often show additional bumps on the head, formed by harmless calcium deposits on their skull.

Giraffe exhibit an unusual walking style, known as pacing, where both legs on the same side move together. They gallop with a different style of locomotion, with front and rear legs moving as pairs, enabling them to reach speeds of 60 kph / 37 mph. They generally sleep on their knees and for

76   Drinking can be a delicate procedure.

What's in a name?
The scientific name *camelopardalis*
derives from the face of a Camel
and pattern like a Leopard.

This female can be identified
by her feathery-tufted horns.

only four to five hours per day, which is considered low in the animal kingdom.

The heart is huge (60 cm / 24" long and weighing 11 kg / 24 lb) and exerts double the pressure of most mammals in order to send blood to the brain. There is a complex system of valves that close when the animal lowers its head, preventing excessive blood pressure damaging the brain.

Courtship and reproduction is cautiously slow and begins when the female is in oestrus. The dominant male carries out urinalysis with his tongue and typically grimaces with a lip-curl at the taste (see *The taste test, page 99*). Usually, a single calf is born and the female takes sole responsibility for its upbringing, sometimes sharing the tasks with other mothers at a crèche, or calving pool.

Generally silent, Giraffe occasionally grunt and bellow, and females whistle to their young if they stray too far. Otherwise, infrasound communication that is beyond human perception is commonly used.

A tall story The question of why a Giraffe has such a long neck has puzzled the greatest minds for centuries. In the 19th Century, Jean-Baptiste Lamarck, an evolutionary theorist, suggested the long neck was an acquired characteristic from previous generations aiming to reach the highest leaves. Charles Darwin agreed with the notion and developed his own competing browsers theory that supported food competition between browsers as the driving force. This theory remained unchallenged for over 150 years but modern research suggests that Darwin's greatest theory of evolution, natural selection, is predominantly responsible. Male Giraffe with the heaviest heads, supported by longer and stronger necks, have the competitive advantage in 'necking' battles (their only form of combat) and mate with more females. Therefore, the forces of sexual selection are dominant over food competition. Stick your neck out – what's your opinion?

These males can be identified by their flat and bare-topped horns.

Cape Buffalo *Syncerus caffer*

Swa: **Nyati or Mbogo**   Maa: **Olarro**

Length: HBT 4·2 m / 14 ft; SH 1·7 m / 5½ ft	
Gestation: 50 weeks.	
Recognition: unmistakable; huge dark cattle with impressive horns and large drooping ears.	
Habits: usually encountered in large family herds, or smaller associations of males.	
Where to find: swamps, savanna and grasslands, and sometimes in forest.	
Feeds on: long grass and rank vegetation.	

The gregarious Cape Buffalo is often wrongly referred to as Water Buffalo, which is an Asiatic species, and is by far the most abundant member of the 'Big Five' in the Masai Mara. It has a reputation for ferocity and has killed many people in Africa over the years – solitary bulls,

This powerful and dangerous animal can be found all over the Mara but it must have access to water and mud. To Maasai people, Buffalo are considered bad luck because they can be very destructive especially the older solitary males that can be very bad tempered and harm many people.   ***Petro Naurori***

weighing up to 1,000 kg / 2,200 lbs, being the most dangerous. In large congregations they can be quite timid, even skittish, often stampeding away from a perceived threat, human or otherwise. Lion (*page 26*) is the major predator of Buffalo but calves may also fall prey to Leopard (*page 30*) and Spotted Hyena (*page 44*). An entire herd will form a tight circle around calves and defend them vigorously, whether related or not. Lions prefer to tackle smaller numbers of male Buffalo rather than face the wrath of a herd of females.

These males can be identified by their fused horns that create a 'boss', as well as the tangle of hair below their belly.

Male

Buffalo often greet visitors on game-drives with stares (like you owe them money!), followed by a roundabout turn, head-tossing and a hasty retreat accompanied by grunts and the tail raised high.

Mature males are very dark-brown to black and often show whitish marks around the eyes. Females tend to be browner, while calves are chestnut-brown for their first few years. A mature bull's horns are fused in the centre, creating a 'boss', making them easily distinguishable from females. The dominant bull is generally the one with the largest horns.

Buffalo are prime ruminants (*see opposite*) and spend much of their day lying down and chewing the cud. Along with Elephant (*page 62*) and Hippo (*page 68*), they are very good at reducing tall grass for selective grazers and their movements may be loosely tracked by gazelle and other herbivores. Large molars crush the grass that is rasped into the mouth using a thick, prehensile tongue.

Buffalo require considerable amounts of water and may spend hours wandering from one source to another during the drier months. This is the period when males break away from the herd to form two types of bachelor group: one for young males aged 3–7 years and another for those aged 11 years and older. The dominant males, aged 8–10 years, generally stay behind to watch over the herd. Younger groups will rejoin the herd upon the onset of rains, while older bulls, unable to compete with the stronger, more virile youngsters may not return at all, preferring to roam together in small numbers – acting like quintessential 'grumpy old men'. Calves are born at the start of the rains and bond closely with their mothers, who are ready for mating with the dominant bull a month or so later.

Ruminants

Ruminants are separated from non-ruminants by their digestive system and, in particular, the presence of four-chambered stomachs. Once plant material has been consumed by a ruminant, it is partially digested in the first stomach, known as the rumen, where bacteria reduce it to a soft mass, known as cud which is later regurgitated and chewed over a second time. This ensures that coarse plant fibres are processed to maximize the calorific and protein yield for the animal. The large herbivores covered on the previous pages, Elephant (*page 62*) to Plains Zebra (*page 72*), are non-ruminants, while the species from Cape Buffalo here to Wildebeest (*page 104*), all are ruminants.

A calf appears much browner than its mother.

A large herd of females which can be identified by their long, slender horns.

Eland *Tragelaphus oryx*

Length: HBT 4·35 m / 14 ft; SH 1·8 m / 6 ft

Gestation: 35–39 weeks.

Recognition: a huge, cattle-like antelope, both sexes bearing large, spiralled horns.

Habits: typically shy and usually trots away from vehicles, most commonly seen in large family herds and smaller same-sex groups.

Where to find: open grasslands, wooded savanna, bushy thickets and acacia scrub.

Feeds on: a browsed diet of herbs and foliage but also grazes.

The largest of all antelope, the Eland is a huge animal comparable in size to oxen, with the largest males exceeding 900 kg / 2,000 lbs in weight, making it almost twice that of the heaviest Greater Kudu (*page 86*). This huge mass hinders the animal when fleeing from danger and they tend to run with a steady trot rather than a dash. Their jumping ability is not affected, however, with well-grown animals well able to clear a 3 m / 10 ft fence! Herds of females and juveniles often exceed 100 in number, while bachelor groups are usually much smaller and led by a dominant male that is darker and greyer than his younger subordinates. This bull also shows the most impressive dewlap, a saggy flap of skin that hangs from the throat, and a matted toupee of hair on the crown of its head. Listen out for the clicking of knee joints as these animals walk; this is assumed to be social adverts within their non-territorial assemblages. Maternal herds are frequently visited by males that seek females in oestrus, testing their urine before mating with those in season. Unlike the young of most other antelope that hide for weeks, newborn Eland join the maternal herd within one day and begin to mingle with other youngsters in a crèche straightaway.

A mixed herd of females and calves.

A mature male showing the pendulous dewlap of skin on his neck.

Older males appear greyer in colour and develop a rusty brown toupe and hindneck.

Greater Kudu *Tragelaphus strepsiceros*

Swa: **Tandala**   Maa: **Emaalo**

Length: HBT 3 m / 10 ft; SH 1·4 m / 4½ ft

Gestation: 39 weeks.

Recognition: a tall, athletic antelope with a grey-brown coat bearing 5–12 narrow white lines down the sides, a spinal crest and a white chevron between the eyes. Adult males have long horns with up to 2½ twists and a shaggy beard.

Habits: active during the cooler hours of the day, retiring to cover in the heat.

Where to find: rocky hillsides with plenty of cover and sometimes acacia scrub.

Feeds on: selectively browsed leaves, shoots, fruits and succulent plants.

This stunning antelope is second in size only to the Eland (*page 84*), with which it shares many features, including numerous narrow white body stripes,

Females lack horns and appear more delicate than the robust males.

long spiralled horns and an amazing ability to jump when in danger. The horns of mature bulls are massive, reaching over 1·85 m / 6 ft in length and are used for fighting other males. During fights horns can get locked together, resulting in the death of both individuals! Kudu prefer to run from predators, such as Lion (*page 26*), Leopard (*page 30*) and Wild Dog (*page 59*). However, although they are very agile sprinters, leaping over high bushes and rocks, they lack stamina and are frequently taken by energetic Wild Dog in particular. A dominant male may preside over several herds, each containing several females and calves. Immature males tend to gather in bachelor groups, whereas non-dominant mature males roam alone.

A stunning mature male with huge, spiralled horns.

Bush Duiker *Sylvicapra grimmia*

Swa: **Nsya**   Maa: **Empanas**

Length: HBT 135 cm / 53"; SH 50 cm / 20"

Gestation: 18–23 weeks.

Recognition: similar to, but slightly larger than, Kirk's Dik-dik (*page 90*) but separated by the small, black, button-nose, dark blaze running down the snout, and the black-striped tail.

Habits: primarily nocturnal in the Mara and very shy, usually solitary or in pairs.

Where to find: prefers dense cover in woodland and forest but occasionally seen in the open.

Feeds on: a browsed diet of leaves, shoots and seeds, fallen fruits and sometimes small animals.

This attractive small antelope has adopted the clever habit of following groups of birds and monkeys feeding in fruiting trees, and waits for fallen fruit to land below. Horn-bearing males are smaller than the hornless females and they live in monogamous pairs. Disturbed animals freeze, just like Kirk's Dik-dik, before diving into deep cover. In fact the name 'duiker' comes from the Afrikaans / Dutch word meaning 'diver' on account of this habit. Not surprisingly, these shy creatures hide their young, and often raise two offspring per year. Males are highly territorial and frequently scent their trails with dung piles and gland secretions on vegetation, and by scratching trees with their horns.

The black blaze on the snout helps to identify the Bush Duiker from other small antelope.

☐ **Oribi** *Ourebia ourebi*

Length: HBT 155 cm / 61"; SH 60 cm / 24"

Gestation: 28 weeks.

Recognition: a slender, tan-coloured antelope with large ears and a clog-shaped head. Both sexes have white eye-rings but only males show narrow, spiky horns.

Habits: avoids the heat of the day but is active early mornings and evenings.

Where to find: uncommon in grasslands and open savanna, most often seen in the southern sector of the Mara.

Feeds on: short grass, though often in areas of long grass.

This tan-coloured, white-bellied antelope has a black spot, or sub-auricular gland, below the ears, as in the similar-looking reedbucks (*pages 92–93*). However, Oribi is easily separated from these species by its smaller size and more slender build. It also shows a distinctive black tip to the short, bushy tail which is flagged-up when running away from predators, in a similar stotting fashion (see *page 92*) to reedbuck. It is when they are threatened that you are likely to hear their main vocalization, a high-pitched, shrill whistle. Like the Bush Duiker, female Oribi give birth in long grass and hide their young for up to two months.

Both sexes show a black spot under the ears but only males sport short, pointed horns.

Kirk's Dik-dik *Madoqua kirkii*

Length: HBT 80 cm / 31"; SH 40 cm / 16"

Gestation: 26 weeks.

Recognition: a delicate grey-brown antelope with a large nose. Both sexes have a crest of erectile hair between the ears and males show short, spiky horns.

Habits: shy and retiring, will freeze at sight or sound of danger.

Where to find: wooded savanna and riverine woodland; particularly fond of Croton thickets.

Feeds on: a variety of leaves and shoots; a choosy browser.

It is widely believed in Maasai culture that if a Dik-dik runs across your path then something bad will happen!
David Lekada Mpusia
[*Maybe this is because a running Dik-dik is often closely followed by a hungry Leopard?*]

This attractive dwarf antelope is common in the Mara and well known among guides for its monogamous behaviour. Active day and night, if you see one, you can be sure there is another close-by. Look out for the classic 'freeze' behaviour, often with a front foot raised. The large, mobile snout is used as a cooling device and is even larger on species of dik-dik found in drier regions. Like the Klipspringer, Kirk's Dik-dik show prominent pre-orbital scenting glands under the eyes that are used to add a sticky secretion to stems that it passes. If you're lucky enough to have Kirk's Dik-dik in the camp you are staying at, also look out for their communal dung heaps that are pawed heavily with scratch marks in the ground.

Note the round pre-orbital gland in front of the eye that is used to lay scent on vegetation.

Klipspringer *Oreotragus oreotragus*

Swa: **Mbuzi mawe**   Maa: **Enkine Oosoito**

Length: HBT 125 cm / 49"; SH 60 cm / 24"

Gestation: 30 weeks.

Recognition: a small, stocky, goat-like antelope with a dark grey-olive coat and short, spiky horns in both sexes. The large, round ears are distinctively patterned on the inside.

Habits: wanders quietly in pairs or small family groups.

Where to find: on rocky outcrops and scree, primarily on the Oloololo Escarpment.

Feeds on: a variety of grasses, herbs and succulent plants.

Meaning 'rock-jumper' in Afrikaans and Dutch, Klipspringer are water independent, able to acquire all the fluids they need from their food. While one animal grazes another will look out for predators, announcing danger with a whistled alarm. Amazingly, they walk on the very tips of their hooves and can balance with all four feet on a rock smaller than an adult human's fist!

The Klipspringer often gives the impression of a small mountain goat.

Mountain Reedbuck *Redunca fulvorufula*   Swa: **Tohe ya milima**   Maa: **Enkakuluo**

Also known as Chanler's Mountain Reedbuck

Length: HBT 162 cm / 64"; SH 75 cm / 30"

Gestation: 32 weeks.

Recognition: darker and greyer above than Bohor Reedbuck with a thicker coat for the cooler conditions at higher altitudes. Females larger than males, the latter showing forward-curving horns.

Habits: most active at dawn and dusk, moving in small herds.

Where to find: well-drained grassy and rocky hillsides.

Feeds on: grasses and herbs.

Unlikely to be encountered away from its preferred habitat of hillside grassland, the Mountain Reedbuck is generally encountered in small groups of 3–7, mostly females overseen by a lone male, or *ram*. It is most common in the north-east of the reserve on the hills near Aitong. When they reach maturity, young males are evicted from the group and form separate bachelor groups, though the two types of group may be seen grazing together during the dry season. The bushy tail is dark above and white below, is used as a flagging signal at sight or sound of danger. Like Bohor Reedbuck and Oribi (*page 89*), this species usually shows an obvious black patch under the ears known as the sub-auricular gland.

Stotting
When threatened with real danger, both reedbuck species run away at speed, leaping into the air with exaggerated rocking bounces to reveal a flash of white under the tail. This behaviour, which is common amongst antelope species, is known as stotting or pronking, and is used as a signal to predators that the animal is healthy and difficult to catch.

Bohor Reedbuck *Redunca redunca*

Swa: **Tohe or Forhi** Maa: **Enkakuluo**

Length: HBT 155 cm / 61"; SH 90 cm / 35"

Gestation: 32 weeks.

Recognition: a heavily-built antelope, tawny-brown above with white underparts. Only males have horns, which are forward-curving.

Habits: tends to hide in vegetation during the day and feed mostly at night.

Where to find: most abundant on floodplains, *e.g.* Musiara, but also in lower densities along narrow river courses with good cover.

Feeds on: grasses, shoots and reed stems.

As with many other antelope species, the male Bohor Reedbuck enjoys the company of several females within his territory and, in prime habitat, may be accompanied by as many as 7 mature females. Both reedbuck species can be separated from other brown antelope by their solid build and large, oval ears. A good view will show the conspicuous dark eyes and nose against the pale face. Bohor Reedbuck is an abundant species in the Mara but can be difficult to observe on account of its habit of lying within long grass in the middle of floodplains. Since this reedbuck prefers to hide rather than run from danger, it is sometimes possible to get very close to them on game-drives. (For more information on reedbuck behaviour, see Mountain Reedbuck *opposite*.)

Both sexes show a black spot under the ears but only males sport short forward-curving horns.

Bushbuck *Tragelaphus scriptus*

Length: HBT 175 cm/69"; SH 80 cm/31"

Gestation: 26–30 weeks.

Recognition: a slim, reddish-brown antelope with a crest on the arched back, often with vertical white stripes down the flanks and numerous white markings on the face. Straight, spiralled horns occur in males only.

Habits: usually shy and elusive but can become tame around camps and lodges where it may be seen at any time of day or night.

Where to find: forest-edge, well-wooded savanna and riverine woodland.

Feeds on: leaves, herbs, seeds and fruits.

This is a medium-sized, elegant antelope that can be difficult to find where it is not habituated to people. The most obvious sign of its presence is the loud gruff "bark" that is used to alert others to a threat nearby, often before it leaps into deep cover with athletic bounds and a white flash of its raised tail. Bushbuck tend to be solitary and non-territorial in nature, staying within a home range that may include many other individuals. However, they may gather in small numbers where resources abound, especially fallen fruits and water. Adults of both sexes are beautifully marked with unique black and white spots and bands on their face, ears, legs and tail; these markings are believed to be used for signalling.

A white-spotted, chestnut coat helps to identify both sexes of Bushbuck.

Defassa Waterbuck *Kobus ellipsiprymnus*

Swa: **Kuru** Maa: **Olmooinko**

Length: HBT 2·8 m / 9 ft; SH 1·4 m / 4½ ft

Gestation: 39–41 weeks.

Recognition: a large, shaggy-looking antelope. Males are dark and show long, curved and heavily-ringed horns, while females are reddish-brown and hornless.

Habits: gregarious, forming large herds of females with young and a few males.

Where to find: common and widespread in open and wooded savanna, often close to water.

Feeds on: mostly grass but sometimes other vegetation.

Waterbuck are not confined to wetlands but do require freshwater for drinking on a regular basis. They prefer medium-length grasslands where they gather in considerable numbers, dominated by a single male that may allow other, subordinate males, to accompany the herd. Otherwise, bachelor herds of young males are found a short distance away from the main herd, frequently engaging in mock-fighting with clashes of horns. It is sometimes claimed that Waterbuck meat is inedible, a myth that stems from the foul-smelling sweat glands under the skin that give the animal's coat a greasy waterproofing. They are less frequently hunted by big cats than other antelopes, possibly because they taste unpleasant. When predators are sighted, Waterbuck will intimidate them by staring and stamping their feet, often giving a loud gruff snort as a warning to others.

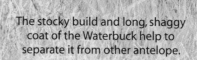

The stocky build and long, shaggy coat of the Waterbuck help to separate it from other antelope.

95

Impala *Aepyceros melampus*

Length: HBT 205 cm / 81"; SH 90 cm / 35"

Gestation: 28 weeks.

Recognition: a slim, elegant antelope with a tan head and upper body, lighter tan layer below and a white belly. There are two vertical narrow black stripes at the rear and the white tail has a black stripe down its length. Only males have the ornate horns.

Habits: most active in the daytime, gathering in large herds.

Where to find: common in wooded savanna and along riverine woodland edge.

Feeds on: very adaptable according to the season. Grazes when grass is green but browses on foliage when grass is brown and dry.

This beautiful antelope is common at the border between woodland and grassland where it grazes in large herds. Groups of females, or *ewes*, known collectively as a harem, and their young, or *fawns*, are dominated by a prime male, or *ram*. A dominant male controls a harem for up to three months, typically two, during which time he fends off other males and shepherds his flock closely to him. During this period, he chases females aggressively, giving prolonged, barked snorts and all the time smelling their scent with curled-up lips. He has sole mating rights with all females coming into oestrus during his reign, ensuring that the strongest genes are passed down within the herd. Nearby, groups of subordinate and young males watch on in bachelor herds, awaiting the opportunity to topple the

Females can always be indentified by their lack of horns.

dominant male who eventually weakens and shows characteristic black eye patches. (After two months of constant mating, chasing and fighting, this is understandable!) Females can delay birthing for up to a month if grazing conditions are poor. Newborn fawns are hidden from danger in long grass for a week before joining the herd, and young animals gather to form their own crèches, supervised by any female that happens to be nearby.

Impala are a favoured prey item of stalking Leopard (*page 30*), racing Cheetah (*page 34*) and packs of Wild Dog (*page 59*) but are usually too fast for Lion (*page 26*) and Spotted Hyena (*page 44*). When startled, the herd splits dramatically, with animals heading in all directions and leaping with impressive jumps of up to 10 m / 35 ft long and 3 m / 10 ft high in order to confuse the predator. At the same time, they release a scent from glands in their rear shins that enable individuals to relocate the herd once danger has passed.

A resplendent adult male Impala showing the double-curved horns that illustrate his age.

Grant's Gazelle *Nanger granti*

Swa: **Swala granti** Maa: **Oloibor siadi**

Length: HBT 190 cm/75"; SH 90 cm/35"

Gestation: 28 weeks.

Recognition: beige back separated from white belly with a dark stripe along the flanks. Both sexes have lyre-shaped, ringed horns which are larger in males. Shows a thicker neck and longer legs than Thomson's Gazelle (*page 100*) and the white 'letter-box' above the tail is best identification feature.

Habits: joins other grazers on the plains after rains but separates during dry periods.

Where to find: open plains and acacia scrub.

Feeds on: grass when green and switches to browsing during dry periods.

This large, elegant gazelle is found in smaller numbers than its diminutive cousin, the Thomson's Gazelle. It is adapted to succeed in dry conditions and while many other antelope head into the Serengeti for greener pastures, the Grant's will head into the dry acacia belt and browse on shoots and herbage, surviving for long periods without water. Unlike Thomson's Gazelle, the male Grant's does not scent-mark with pre-orbital glands (*page 90*) but scents using shin glands and dung sites for territory marking. Males defend their patch by intimidation displays, swinging their strong necks from side to side. Females crossing into defended territories are enticed by the male's prancing courtship dance with his nose in the air and tail raised.

From behind, Grant's Gazelle always show a white 'letter-box' just above the tail.

The taste test

Many male animals, from cats to Giraffe, employ a strange habit of testing for whether a female is in oestrus (*i.e.* fertile) by, in most cases, smelling or, in some species such as Giraffe, even tasting her urine. This urinalysis is based on minute pheromone changes which can be identified by the vomeronasal organ located at the top of the mouth. During the analysis, the animal doing the testing grimaces, often with the top lip curled upwards, a reaction known as the Flehman response.

What's in a name?

Both gazelle species were named after Scottish explorers: Grant (1827–1892), who accompanied Speke on his quest for the 'Source of the Nile'; and Thomson (1858–1895), who travelled overland from the Tanzanian coast to Lake Victoria and authored the travelogue *Through Masai Land*.

The stripe along the flanks of a male vary from pale to dark-brown, but are never black like the Thomson's Gazelle.

Females show thin, delicate horns compared to those of the male.

Thomson's Gazelle *Eudorcas thomsonii*   Swa: **Swala tomi**   Maa: **Enkolii or Enkoperai**

Length: HBT 150 cm/59"; SH 70 cm/28"

Gestation: 24–25 weeks.

Recognition: dark tan on the back, extending to the tail, and white below with a bold black stripe along the flanks. Males have slightly curved, ringed horns, while females show two short spikes.

Habits: a communal grazer that mixes well with other herbivores.

Where to find: short grass plains.

Feeds on: predominantly short grass but may browse herbage when grass is dry.

Widely known as the 'Tommie', this charming small gazelle is common and widespread across short grass plains. Although resident in many areas, large numbers migrate into the Mara from the Serengeti from July onwards, following Wildebeest (*page 104*) and Plains Zebra (*page 72*). They benefit from the lawnmower-effect of these larger grazers that reduces the longer grass to greening shoots. Adults keep within eye contact of each other and use tail-wagging as a means of communication. Females move extensively in loose groups, passing through the territories of numerous males as they travel. The dominant males defend their territories from intruding males with rapid charges and sometimes horn clashes. Although jackals (*pages 56–57*) and Spotted Hyena (*page 44*) readily take newborn gazelle, the Cheetah (*page 34*) is the adults' major predator. Although slower than Grant's Gazelle (*page 98*), which can usually outrun Cheetah, the smaller Tommie is capable of high-speed jinks and turns which may sometimes save it. When confronted by the slower Lion (*page 26*) or Spotted Hyena, most gazelle perform stotting and pronking manoeuvres (see *page 92*) to display their fitness and agility.

From behind, Thomson's Gazelle always show rusty brown above the tail, unlike the Grant's Gazelle.

Gazelle birth and threats

Female gazelle leave the herd to give birth, often in tall grass. The afterbirth is eaten immediately and the newborn is licked so the mother's scent is fixed on the fawn. Although the fawn can stand within minutes of birth, the mother leaves it for several hours, reducing the risk of drawing attention to it and returns later to nurse the fawn. Most fawns will remain hidden for several days, sometimes weeks with Grant's Gazelle, before joining up with mother and the rest of the herd.

This calf is just a few hours old.

Both sexes show a distinctive pattern from the side – a white belly below a black stripe, above which is a beige stripe and then the rusty-brown back.

Females show very small horns compared to males.

Even though they are very common animals in the Masai Mara, I still really enjoy watching young gazelle play and chase each other around. It is vital training for the young and such fun to watch.

Petro Naurori

Coke's Hartebeest *Alcelaphus buselaphus*

Swa: **Kongoni** Maa: **Olkondi**

Length: HBT 2·85 m / 9½ ft; SH 1·5 m / 5 ft

Gestation: 34½ weeks.

Recognition: similar to Topi but the body colour is paler brown with off-white buttocks and rear legs. The distinctive horns curve out before curling back in.

Habits: a scarce and shy antelope often found in small family groups.

Where to find: open and wooded savanna.

Feeds on: a selective grazer on medium-height grass and herbage.

The Hartebeest is a widely distributed African species with many local variations and regional subspecies.

The subspecies found in the Mara and much of southern Kenya and northern Tanzania is *A.b.cokii* and is known as Coke's Hartebeest. Hartebeest are often encountered in longer grass than their darker cousin, the Topi, and their behaviour is less energetic. Males will often engage in sniffing and nibbling the neck of a competitor in advance of a territorial challenge. Hartebeest and Topi are structurally very similar, showing strong forequarters and a sloping back to lower rear quarters.

What's in a name?
The name is a corruption of *hert*, the Afrikaans and Dutch word for deer.

Compared to the Topi, Hartebeest always appear very pale on the rear.

Topi *Damaliscus lunatus*

Length: HBT 2·72 m / 9 ft; SH 1·25 m / 4 ft

Gestation: 34½ weeks.

Recognition: Smaller and darker than Hartebeest, with a chestnut-tan coat. Shows distinctive dark patches on the upper leg and mustard-coloured patches on the lower leg. The back is strongly angled and the horn shape is unique.

Habits: A sociable antelope often found standing on a termite-mound looking for threats, sleeping with muzzle touching the ground, or running vigorously.

Where to find: Short to medium length grassland and savanna.

Feeds on: A selective grazer of fresh green shoots and herbage.

The graceful Topi is a socially organised antelope with groups adjusting their behaviour according to the size of the herd. In the Mara, where sizeable resident groups gather, males establish territories that include a number of mature females and their young. These females take this 'honour' very seriously and will chase off intruding Topi of both sexes.

Groups of bachelor males gather at communal display areas, known as leks, where they establish a rank of dominance involving energetic fighting, usually on bended knee, with victors chasing losers away at speeds of up to 70 kph / 43 mph. This speed also enables them to outrun most predators, and Spotted Hyena (*page 44*) prefer to stalk them while they sleep.

A dominant male Topi will work hard to see off rivals for the privilege of mating rights to his harem of females. Throughout March and April, he performs elegant prancing and high-stepping dances with his tail raised to court them, and engages in rear-end sniffing at regular intervals. He must get his timing right as females are in oestrus for just one day in the entire year. Around eight months later, usually in October, she gives birth to an energetic youngster that remains by her side for a whole year.

Topi are frequently seen with mud-decorated horns and this may be how they acquired their name (the Kiswahili word for mud is *matope*, pronounced *ma-toe-pay*).

☐ White-bearded Wildebeest *Connochaetes taurinus*   Swa: **Nyumbu**   Maa: **Oinkat**

Also known as Gnu

Length: HBT 3·4 m / 11 ft; SH 1·4 m / 4½ ft

Gestation: 35–39 weeks.

Recognition: a stocky antelope with a short, thick neck, spindly legs and smooth, curved horns. The glossy, grey-brown coat is variable in tone and shade but usually shows numerous darker stripes and a black face mask contrasting with an off-white, flowing beard.

Habits: typically found in herds of 100s or 1,000s, it mixes well with Plains Zebra (*page 72*), and wanders constantly in search of fresh pasture and water.

Where to find: open plains of long and short grass, acacia scrub and wooded savanna.

Feeds on: an exclusive diet of grass, with a preference for short grass.

The Wildebeest is a strange-looking creature by anyone's standards, but its lifestyle is so impressive that it attracts hundreds of thousands of visitors to the Mara each year. Most tourists visit with high hopes of witnessing the spectacle of large numbers of animals crossing the mighty Mara River. However, even the sight and sound of huge numbers grazing on the open plains is breathtaking.

Life for Wildebeest is one of perpetual motion; within minutes of birth they are walking and they barely stop for the rest of their lives. They are driven to wander by the need for fresh green grass and fresh water and are perfectly designed to be nature's lawnmowers. When not walking in convoy, or pausing to look out for danger, the broad muzzle is kept low to the ground where it continuously takes large

Serengeti Wildebeest.

The Mara-Serengeti ecosystem is dependant upon the two Wildebeest migrations which are, in turn, dictated by the rains. While the migration pathway of the Serengeti Wildebeest is secure, the migration corridors used by the Loita population along with the many Zebra and gazelle that travel with them, is under threat from agricultural development and human settlement. This is one of the reasons we worked so hard to establish the Naboisho Conservancy, so that we could protect the natural corridors used by this important migration of animals.

Jackson Looseyia

bites of grass. Compared to other grazers, Wildebeest have a wider row of front teeth, or incisors, that rasp everything that enters the bite zone. The effect of one-and-a-half million lawnmowers is enormous and, when combined with the fertilizer (*i.e.* dung and urine) that they return to the ground, it is easy to understand why they have a huge influence in maintaining the landscape of the Mara-Serengeti ecosystem.

The Wildebeest migration begins at birth in the southern Serengeti, usually on the Ndutu Plains in February. The breeding strategy is such that around 85% of all calves are born within a three-week period. This ensures that predators, such as Lion (*page 26*), Leopard (*page 30*), Cheetah (*page 34*) and Spotted Hyena (*page 44*), are overwhelmed by the vast amount of food available. Furthermore, calving starts at dawn and is usually completed by midday, causing a huge glut in numbers that cannot be harvested quickly enough by the carnivores. Within 3 minutes of birth, a calf is on its feet and able to follow its mother. Unlike most other antelope that hide their young in the grass for

Loita Wildebeest.

weeks (*i.e.* they are 'hiders'), Wildebeest adopt a 'follower' system, in keeping with their wandering lifestyle. Experienced mothers are more successful in rearing their young than new mothers, which have an unfortunate habit of forgetting their calves and consequently losing them to predation. Mother and calf will remain together for a full year and are able to recognize each others' calls and locate each other within a vast, noisy herd if they become separated.

Due to the inherent mobility of the herds and fluctuations in resource availability, Wildebeest do not hold permanent territories or create pair-bonds. Instead, they indulge in a mating season frenzy, called the rut, when males set up temporary territories on the best patches of ground wherever they happen to arrive in early June. It is at this time, after the long rains, that most animals are at their physical peak. These rutting grounds hold approximately 250,000 grunting and prancing males vying for the attention of over 750,000 females. Each male endeavours to entice the females passing close to him, while also attempting to defend his chosen spot against other males,

usually with a threatening lowering of horns. The odds are stacked against young and inexperienced males but this strategy ensures that the fittest and healthiest individuals get to pass on their genes. The best 'honker' usually wins!

As the Wildebeest begin to arrive into the Mara from the Serengeti, around July, they are usually seen in vast herds, mixed with many Plains Zebra (*page 72*) and Thomson's Gazelle (*page 100*). Both these species benefit from following a large Wildebeest herd as it clears vast swathes of tall grass, opening it up for better grazing – and all benefit from increased vigilance against the predators that await them on the open plains.

The population of Wildebeest appears relatively stable over recent years but they have experienced some major lows in the past. In the late 1800s, the viral disease *Rinderpest* spread through introduced cattle into the Wildebeest herds and reduced their population to around 200,000. Today, *Rinderpest* has been eliminated but Wildebeest are increasingly threatened by illegal hunting in Tanzania, where they are currently being poached at a rate of 20,000 per year.

It's rare to see a Wildebeest calf this young in the Masai Mara. This one was photographed in the Ngorongoro Crater in March.

What's in a name?

Wildebeest derive their name from the Afrikaans for 'wild cattle', while Gnu is a Khoi Khoi (Hottentot) name for the animal, stemming from their call "*ga-noo*". The scientific name *Connochaetes* derives from the ancient Greek for 'beard of white flowing hair'.

The 'Serengeti' herd arriving at Bila Shaka in August.

Cape Hare *Lepus capensis*

Swa: **Sunkura**   Maa: **Enkitonjo**

Length: HBT 65 cm / 26"	
Gestation: 6 weeks.	
Recognition: identified from Scrub Hare by the heavily grizzled grey-brown coat that lacks warm tones.	
Habits: nocturnal and rarely seen in the daytime except when flushed from dense grassland.	
Where to find: open grasslands and open savanna, avoiding wet floodplains and bushy scrub.	
Feeds on: mostly grasses but also shrubs and herbs.	

These two hares are very similar in appearance but identification based on habitat preference is fairly reliable. Both show a black-and-white tail, which is flashed as a warning to others when running at speed – although both species prefer to hide from danger rather than run. Their huge, long ears separate them immediately from the similar Springhare and their front legs are only half the length of the rear legs. Unlike the Springhare, these true hares do not dig a burrow but sleep in a grassy hollow, known as a form, during the day.

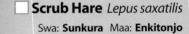

Scrub Hare *Lepus saxatilis*

Swa: **Sunkura**   Maa: **Enkitonjo**

Length: HBT 60 cm / 24"	
Gestation: 6 weeks.	
Recognition: identified from Cape Hare by the contrasty facial pattern, warm rusty tones, particuarly to the back of the neck and, often, a white spot on the forehead.	
Habits: mostly nocturnal but frequently seen during the cooler hours of the day, often close to bushy cover.	
Where to find: common at the grassland edge, in woody thickets and acacia scrub, even close to Maasai villages.	
Feeds on: mostly grasses but also other plants.	

Springhare *Pedetes capensis*

Swa: **Kamendegere**   Maa: **Enkipuldiany**

Length: HBT 90 cm / 35"

Gestation: 11 weeks.

Recognition: looks like a small kangaroo with massive hindlegs, tiny front legs and a long, bushy black-tipped tail.

Habits: strictly nocturnal, emerging from sheltered burrows after sunset to feed on grasslands.

Where to find: bushy scrub and open grasslands.

Feeds on: a variety of plant matter including grasses and herbs.

This bizarre nocturnal creature is actually a rodent, not a hare. It looks just like a kangaroo and behaves like one too – being able to jump in excess of 2 m / 6 ft in a bound and to travel very fast when threatened. Springhare have scruffy long claws on the very long rear legs that it uses for digging and traction, but the front legs are tiny and barely used at all. Their eyes are huge and provide exceptional night-vision, and the senses of smell and hearing are acute. The Springhare has one of the lowest reproductive rates among rodents, with just a single young born at a time. It does, however, usually breed twice, and sometimes three times, each year.

Unstriped
Ground
Squirrel

Unstriped Ground Squirrel
Xerus rutilus

Swa: **Kidiri**   Maa: **Karbobo**

Length: HBT 45 cm / 18"
Gestation: 5 weeks.
Recognition: a plain, reddish-brown squirrel with an unmarked, greyish tail.
Habits: diurnal, usually in small groups sharing communal burrows.
Where to find: prefers much drier habitats than the Striped Ground Squirrel, especially in the acacia zone.
Feeds on: a variety of nuts, fruits and seeds, occasionally invertebrates.

Striped Ground Squirrel
Xerus erythropus

Swa: **Kidiri miraba**   Maa: **Karbobo**

Length: HBT 60 cm / 24"
Gestation: 5 weeks.
Recognition: a warm-brown squirrel with a bold white stripe along the body and obvious bars through the tail.
Habits: diurnal and gregarious, often in colonies of up to 30, frequently around termite hills.
Where to find: wooded savanna and rocky areas.
Feeds on: a variety of nuts and seeds, and occasionally invertebrates.

Unlike most other squirrels you might be familiar with, ground squirrels live up to their name and rarely venture into trees. Litters of up to four young are common and family groups communicate with "chitters" and "squeaks", often standing erect with tails flicking.

Striped
Ground
Squirrel

☐ **Grass Rat** *Arvicanthis niloticus*

Swa: **Panya**　Maa: **Enderoni**

Also known as Bush Rat or Acacia Rat

Length: HBT 20–35 cm / 8–14"	
Gestation: 18–25 days.	
Recognition: a nondescript brown mouse with indistinct dark streaking on the back and pale rings around the eyes.	
Habits: diurnal; lives in busy colonies, usually burrowing under an acacia root.	
Where to find: common in the dry acacia zone, often close to human habitation.	
Feeds on: grasses, leaves, shoots & seeds.	

Actually a mouse, rather than a rat, this is probably the most abundant and frequently seen of all small rodents in the Mara. As with many other mice, they are short-lived (two years is a fine old age) but produce up to twelve young several times a year in a labyrinth-like burrow system. They are a favoured prey of many small carnivores, reptiles and predatory birds.

Look out for the males' unfeasibly large testicles, which are the largest of all the animals in the Mara in relation to body size.

Also known as Four-toed Hedgehog or African Pygmy Hedgehog

Length: HBT 25 cm / 10"
Gestation: 5 weeks.
Recognition: upperparts are covered in short, cream-tipped spines and both the underparts and head are white.
Habits: solitary and nocturnal, hiding from heat during the day.
Where to find: savanna, acacia scrub and rocky semi-desert.
Feeds on: mostly invertebrates, including scorpions, but also fruits.

Unlike the Porcupine, the White-bellied Hedgehog holes-up during dry summer periods, a process known as aestivation. This is thought to be in response to food shortages rather than high temperatures *per se* and usually lasts no longer than two months. Females are fertile throughout the year and give birth to a litter of four to five pups, each covered in a fine silky membrane which covers the soft spines and ensures the females are not injured when giving birth. The spines harden within a few days.

This insectivore is vaguely similar to the Crested Porcupine in appearance but is far smaller. Unlike the Porcupine, the very sharp spines, not quills, do not detach upon impact with a predator. Instead, the animal often curls into a ball if severely threatened, making some snorts and whistles of intimidation.

This prickly creature is considered by the Maasai to bring good luck. When a Maasai finds one, he will place it in the centre of his sheep pen and allow the sheep to trample the unfortunate animal to death. After the job is done it is said that his sheep will multiply to the number of spikes on its back! ***Jackson Looseyia***

Length: HBT 90 cm / 35"	
Gestation: 10 weeks.	
Recognition: a large, robust rodent with a thick neck covered in a long grey-haired mane. The upperparts are covered in very long white-tipped black quills.	
Habits: a nocturnal wanderer, sleeping in a burrow during the day.	
Where to find: forest, savanna and dry scrub.	
Feeds on: mostly roots and tubers, but also fruit, invertebrates and rarely carrion.	

This is the largest rodent in East Africa and famous for the impressive array of long, detachable quills on its back. Contrary to local legend, the Porcupine cannot 'shoot' these weapons at predators but it is certainly capable of defending itself by charging, in reverse, at Spotted Hyena (*page 44*), Leopard (*page 30*) and Lion (*page 26*). Even humans have fallen victim and been stabbed by annoyed Porcupines! More common is the threat display which starts with a loud hiss-like rattle, produced by hollow quills near the tail, followed by all quills raised into an impressive crest to make the animal appear much bigger than it really is. Emerging from burrows at dusk, these animals travel great distances in search of food, much of which is dug up using long claws. Family groups, consisting of a monogamous pair and their 1–2 offspring are occasionally encountered at night. Unfortunately, many Porcupine are killed by people as they are considered a pest to crops.

Bush Hyrax *Heterohyrax brucei*

Swa: **Perere mawe or Pimbi**   Maa: **Enkijujur**

Also known as Yellow-spotted Rock Hyrax

Length: HBT 60 cm / 24"

Gestation: 28 weeks.

Recognition: squat and furry, resembling a guinea pig, with long whiskers.

Habits: diurnal and communal, often seen relaxing among trees and rocks.

Where to find: common along forest edge and on rocky outcrops.

Feeds on: mostly leaves, grasses and seeds but also fond of bark, fruits and insects.

This mammal may not win any prizes for its appearance, but it is fascinating to watch and understand in so many ways. It is the closest living relative of the Elephant to be found on land (although recent DNA-analysis suggests that aquatic manatees and dugongs – collectively known as sea-cows or Sirenians – are even more closely related to the Elephant). In general outward appearance, the Hyrax looks similar to a rodent but internally is quite dissimilar. It has a multi-chambered stomach, like a ruminant (see *page 83*), in which bacteria break down plant fibre. Like Elephant, the male Hyrax does not possess a scrotum but keeps its testicles within a cavity close to the kidneys. Females have a pair of teats close to the armpits and have an additional four in the groin area. Although the Hyrax has well-developed incisor teeth, these are not used for browsing, as in rodents. The four lower incisors are used like a

The collective noun for Hyrax is a herd.

comb for sociable grooming, while the top two form rudimentary tusks. Instead, food is grasped by the molars at the rear of the mouth, where it is chewed repeatedly.

Hyrax are considered to be one of the earliest forms of mammal and exhibit some prehistoric features, in particular their poorly developed ability to thermoregulate. This means that groups of Hyrax must huddle together for warmth and bask like reptiles before they are able to become mobile. However, since most Hyrax spend around 95% of the day resting, this habit doesn't disrupt a busy schedule. They are communal creatures that live in a male-dominated harem society. Communal latrines are used as territory markers, often staining trees and rocks with a metallic sheen that is caused by crystallised calcium carbonate in the urine.

Bush Hyrax seem equally at home in the trees as they are among rocks.

■ Greater Galago
Otolemur crassicaudatus

Swa: **Komba ya miombo**
Maa: **Kimaongu**

Length: HBT 85 cm / 33"	

Gestation: 18 weeks.

Recognition: cat-sized and thick-furred with a long, bushy tail. Usually grey-brown in colour although all-black individuals also occur.

Habits: strictly nocturnal and occasionally visits night-time feeding stations at camps and lodges.

Where to find: wooded savanna, thick bush and acacia scrub.

Feeds on: fruits, seeds, tree sap/gum, invertebrates and, rarely, small birds and their eggs.

Separated from the Lesser Galago by its large size, the Greater Galago is frequently seen on the ground, when it stands upright and leaps with hands and bushy tail raised. When in trees, it frequently walks along branches but is a very capable jumper. Unlike the Lesser Galago, females of this species may be seen carrying young jockey-style on their backs.

Bushbaby Basics

Like humans, monkeys and apes, galagos are primates but theirs is a separate and more ancient family. They are very agile in the trees, jumping from one branch to another with great accuracy thanks to exceptional eyesight. They forage alone but communicate with very loud cries, which is why they are often called 'bushbabies', and have excellent hearing thanks to their large, rotating ears. Scent trails are laid with urine and by using scent glands on their chest. They have excellent grasping ability but cannot move their digits independently like other primates. Societies are female-led, with males having smaller territories within the home range of a female collective that often gather to sleep in communal nests or tree-holes.

■ Lesser Galago
Galago senegalensis

Swa: **Komba ndogo**
Maa: **Kimaongu**

Length: HBT 40 cm / 16"	
Gestation: 16–17 weeks.	
Recognition: smaller than a squirrel, with a short, furry coat, a slender tail and a distinctive face pattern.	
Habits: strictly nocturnal and always keeps to the trees, unlike Greater Galago.	
Where to find: prefers dry acacia scrub with scattered large trees.	
Feeds on: mostly tree sap/ gum, fruits, seeds, and small invertebrates.	

These gremlin-like mammals are great fun to watch as they jump among the trees at night. They are a favourite prey item of owls and genets – if they can catch them! Females may be seen carrying their young in their mouths and depositing them on a safe branch before feeding.

Guereza Colobus *Colobus guereza*

Length: HBT 160 cm / 63"

Gestation: 25 weeks.

Recognition: a large black-and-white monkey with a long pendulous tail and a draping mantle of long white hair.

Habits: diurnal and gregarious, mostly active in the middle and upper branches of mature trees.

Where to find: mature forest with secondary growth, the best site being Siana Springs camp.

Feeds on: mostly fresh leaves but also seeds, flowers, fruits and small invertebrates.

This beautiful primate spends most of its time in the trees, where it rests, grooms and feeds for much of the day. It may also be seen walking along the ground, especially when fallen fruit is plentiful. However, fresh green leaves are the preferred diet, and individuals eat approximately one third of their body weight in leaves every day. Groups move between trees with huge leaps, and bound along branches like giant squirrels. Family units are based around a harem of up to ten females and young, all dominated by a single male that will mate with any female. Aggression towards other males is usually shown by chasing and vocalizing but rarely results in physical contact. Young are born with pink skin covered in white hair and rarely stray far from their mother. The contact call of the Guereza Colobus is one of the greatest sounds of East Africa: a huge, deep, croaking "*ruurrrr*" that travels for several kilometres.

The flowing white hair of the Guereza help to make it one of Africa's most attractive primates.

Red-tailed Monkey *Cercopithecus ascanius*

Length: HBT 145 cm / 57"

Gestation: 34½ weeks.

Recognition: has a long, red tail and a pretty face with white cheeks and a white spot on the nose.

Habits: diurnal and gregarious, active in the shady canopy of evergreen trees.

Where to find: forests in the west of the reserve.

Feeds on: leaves, fruits and flowers, rarely invertebrates.

This attractive little monkey is often found in association with other primate species, especially the Blue Monkey (*page 122*), and each benefits from the extra vigilance for predators. As with the Blue Monkey, females without their own young will often take care of their sister's or auntie's young, a behaviour known as alloparenting. This helps to build bonds between the troop females and also gives younger, inexperienced females an opportunity to learn the necessary skills for later life. The Red-tailed Monkey is part of a complex group of *Cercopithecus* monkeys that range across sub-Saharan Africa. The relationship between the different forms is unclear, many being treated as subspecies by some authorities and full species by others.

The white nose and cheeks of the Red-tailed Monkey stand out even when the tail is not visible.

**Blue Monkey ×
Red-tailed Monkey**
The forest of Kichwa Tembo has one individual that is an obvious hybrid, displaying the large body of a Blue Monkey and a demure white-nosed face like a Red-tailed. I am not aware of these two species interbreeding anywhere else.
Joseph Ole Kima

Blue Monkey *Cercopithecus mitis*

Swa: **Kima or Nchima**   Maa: **Olkalou**

Also known as Sykes's Monkey or Gentle Monkey

Length: HBT 170 cm/67"

Gestation: 21 weeks.

Recognition: a solid-looking monkey with a very long tail. The mostly grey-olive coat has some light blue fur on the back, and the face is dark.

Habits: diurnal and gregarious, active in the shady canopy of evergreen trees.

Where to find: forest and riverine woodland within savanna.

Feeds on: leaves, fruits and flowers, rarely invertebrates.

This sombre-looking primate is most often encountered in the forests of the western Mara, especially around Kichwa Tembo camp, but young males looking for new territories wander widely and can turn up almost anywhere with tall trees. Like many other small monkeys, they live in family groups of up to 30, all led by a single dominant male, who is much larger than females. He will not tolerate other males in his territory, even his own offspring. Otherwise, troops are very sociable and spend many hours a day grooming each other. This species has a rich vocabulary with particular calls for specific purposes; this includes a soft "*piaow*" for contact, "*jack!*" for threats, and a deep "*boom*" is produced by the dominant male as a territory marker.

The black cap and
long, dark tail help
to identify the
Blue Monkey even
when the pale
blue-grey back
cannot be seen.

Vervet Monkey *Chlorocebus pygerythrus*

Also known as Savanna Monkey

Swa: **Tumbili** Maa: **Nayo kutuk**

Length: HBT 135 cm / 53"

Gestation: 23½ weeks.

Recognition: the body colour is olive-grey and the face black surrounded by a white rim. This is an agile monkey with a long tail. Adult males show a distinctive powder-blue scrotum.

Habits: a diurnal monkey, at home in trees and grassland. Moves with a bounding gallop along the ground with tail raised.

Where to find: savanna and riverine woodland.

Feeds on: mostly a vegetarian diet of fruits, leaves, seeds and flowers but also takes invertebrates and the eggs and young of birds.

The Vervet is a sociable monkey found in troops of up to 60. These gatherings are highly territorial and both sexes defend against unwelcome intruders. Even competing males from within the troop will collaborate to deny access to outsiders. Otherwise, the troop is a harmonious place where eating and grooming takes up most of the day and young monkeys get to play and develop their communication skills. The Vervet has a distinct language of its own, primarily used to alert other members of the troop to predators. If young monkeys make the correct call for 'air' or 'land' threats they are positively reinforced, but get punished if they give the wrong call. The commonly heard danger call, a barked "*ra-owp*", is used to warn of Leopard (*page 30*).

There's no mistaking a male Vervet Monkey.

124

Monkey business

Grooming is a vital social tool used to cement relationships in both Vervet Monkey and Olive Baboon (*page 126*) troops. Each troop comprises many females and young with fewer males – typically one mature male to every three females. Within a troop there is a complex social hierarchy and just by watching patiently, you should be able to deduce which are the dominant males and females. Females remain with the troop for life, where their dominance is hereditary, but adolescent males are evicted from the troop ensuring they never breed with female relatives.

Olive Baboon *Papio anubis*

Swa: **Nyani**   Maa: **Oyekenyi**

Length: HBT 180 cm / 71"

Gestation: 26 weeks.

Recognition: a large, olive-grey monkey with a long, dog-like muzzle. The eyes are small and set under a heavy eye-brow, and the fairly long tail shows a distinct kink near the base.

Habits: often encountered in large troops either feeding, grooming or just on patrol.

Where to find: quite at home in open grassland, wooded areas and rocky escarpments.

Feeds on: almost anything from bulbs and seeds to invertebrates, sometimes taking birds and mammals to the size of small antelope.

What's in a name? The scientific name *anubis* derives from the Egyptian god of the same name that was represented by a dog's head, similar to that of the Baboon.

Large troops of Olive Baboon are often encountered on game drives but many vehicles pass them by in search of something more

Top tip: avoid standing under Baboons roosting in trees as they habitually shower intruders with liquid excrement!

'exciting'. However, watching Baboons can be very rewarding, so do stop and enjoy! Firstly, check out the males' canine teeth – at 5 cm / 2·5" they are formidable 'weapons' that allow the gangs to wander the plains without harassment. Even Lion (*page 26*) prides will think twice about tackling Baboons. The biggest threat to young Baboons is from the air, where Martial Eagle soar, and a complex vocabulary exists to warn of any threats. Leopard (*page 30*) enjoy eating primates and may attempt to tackle an unsuspecting individual on the edge of the troop and face the wrath of 50 others in hot pursuit.

However, the 'Leopard-bark', a loud "*WA-hooo*", is among the most commonly heard of all Baboon vocalizations.

Also look out for females with pink, swollen rumps (perineal swellings), something that male Baboons get very excited about as it means the females are ready for mating. Even lower ranking males get the chance to mate and often spend more time with younger females, forging a close relationship, or 'consortship' that pays-off when she is ready to mate. If a female isn't receiving as much attention as she needs during this time, she will advertise by 'lip-smacking' and flashing her eyelids at passing males (sound familiar?). There is much fighting between prime troop males, all seeking to control females and food resources, and submission is acknowledged by a 'fear-grin'. Older males are more relaxed and adopt a Godfather-style role with infants – although, as a general rule, Olive Baboons do not engage in cooperative caring of infants. The young usually stick close to their mother at all times, clinging onto her underside when she moves and, after three months, by riding jockey-style on her back.

Baboons' ranges cover vast areas and one of the reasons they are so successful is their ability to adapt to a wide range of environments. Foraging for food occupies much of their day, and they consume almost everything they encounter. During periods of drought, Baboons will even resort to digging up nutrient-rich rhizomes. This may be supplemented by catching small mammals, especially young gazelle, although this is primarily a male-dominated behaviour that is passed down the generational line.

Mature male Baboons tend to walk with a swagger of arrogance.

Reptiles

Nile Crocodile *Crocodylus niloticus*

Length: HBT up to 7·9 m / 26 ft

Recognition: a long, heavily scaled reptile with a long tail, broad snout and obvious teeth. Colour may be grey, brown or olive green with black patches.

Habits: a mostly nocturnal feeder but will attempt to take mammals and fish in daylight.

Where to find: rivers and sometimes large marshes.

Feeds on: insects when very young, moving on to fish and aquatic reptiles, birds and carrion. Large Crocodiles will routinely kill mammals such as Wildebeest and Zebra, and attacks on mature Elephants are well-documented.

Crocodiles are easiest to watch when basking on the sides of rivers to regulate their body temperature. This is the best time to admire their armour-plated leathery skin, which is covered by toughened scales (or scutes) down the

What's in a name? The scientific name derives from the Ancient Greek *kroko~* meaning pebble and *~deilos* meaning worm; *niloticus* refers to the River Nile.

back and tail. The many teeth, variable in size and length, are perfect for grasping and tearing apart their food. The ears, eyes and nostrils are set on the top of the head, allowing an animal to be 99% submerged but still be able to see, smell and breathe. The Nile Crocodile of the Mara River are among the largest remaining in Africa today and frequently exceed 6 m / 20 ft in length and 1,000 kg / 2,200 lbs in weight, and can live to over 100 years old. This is thanks to the annual abundance of meat when Wildebeest (*page 104*) and Plains Zebra (*page 72*) cross the Mara River during the Great Migration. Many animals are killed by Crocodiles, which drown their prey and keep the corpse underwater to soften it. However, many more animals simply drown in the act of crossing. The Mara and Talek Rivers are also home to huge catfish, which Crocodiles herd into the shallows and catch in their powerful jaws. Due to their ectothermic metabolism, Crocodiles can survive for months without food. This is just as well, as the plains game heads into the Serengeti for 8 months of the year. Crocodiles will generally stay submerged for just a few minutes but if they choose to sleep underwater, they can reduce their heart rate and remain there for two hours.

Male Crocodiles mature at around the age of 10, by which time they have reached about 3 m / 10 ft in length; females of a similar age are 30% smaller. Mature males become increasingly territorial and court the females in their area. Mating takes place in the water, after which the female searches for a quiet, sandy bank where she lays an average of 50 eggs in a shallow hole. The ambient temperature determines the sex of the young: above 30˚C (86˚F) creates males and below 30˚C females. The adult female fasts for three months while the young develop, watching out for marauding monitor lizards (*page 132*). Upon hearing the high-pitched calls of the young before they hatch, she will return to help dig them out. Like many birds, hatchlings are born with an egg-tooth, which helps them crack out of their shell.

Once they hatch, the young head straight for the water. The 30 cm / 12" mini-crocs face a huge test for survival as they are favoured prey of the African Fish Eagle and Yellow-billed Stork. They immediately embark on a predatory lifestyle of their own, catching frogs and insects, and grow an average of 30 cm / 12" a year.

Strangely enough, it is widely considered that Crocodiles are more closely related to modern birds than modern lizards, as they share many common features, including a four-chambered heart, rather than a three-chambered heart as in other reptiles.

Top fact: ever wonder about the expression 'crocodile tears'? Just like humans, crocodiles possess lachrymal glands that produce real tears. These are not emotionally driven, however, but act like eye-drops to cleanse the eyes.

Savanna Monitor *Varanus albigularis*

Swa: **Kenge** Maa: **Olmaima**

Also known as the Rock Monitor, this is the heaviest lizard in Africa. Although similar to the Nile Monitor, the head is a very different shape, with a bulbous snout and higher forehead. It can swim well but is far less likely to be encountered in the water than the Nile Monitor.

Monitors are strong, muscular lizards with tough leathery skin and a close view reveals many bead-like scales. They are generally sluggish creatures that amble along with their long, forked tongues flicking and 'tasting' the air for food. When threatened or disturbed, they run very fast with a distinct swagger and raise their hefty bodies clear of the ground.

Nile Monitor *Varanus niloticus*

Swa: **Buru kenge** Maa: **Olmaima**

This is the longest lizard in Africa. It is an excellent swimmer and frequently catches fish underwater. Its distinctive writhing, snake-like motion in the water can be a good feature to separate it from small crocodiles. The raised eyes and nostrils are good indicators of the Nile Monitor's aquatic nature.

Trying to catch monitors is very dangerous as they can cut deeply into the skin with their sharp claws, knock grown men over with a hard smack of the tail and bite very hard and painfully despite their blunt teeth. As monitors routinely feed on decaying matter, they often carry the toxic bacterium *Clostridium botulinum* that causes Botulism, a paralysing and often fatal illness. Bizarrely, this is the same toxin used in Botox cosmetic surgery.

Length: HBT 200 cm / 6½ ft

Recognition: variable but most are dark grey with some light barring on the body and tail, and a pale throat. The head is shorter and broader than that of Nile Monitor.

Habits: usually encountered on the ground but also climbs trees.

Where to find: open and wooded savanna, especially with termite mounds.

Feeds on: a variety of invertebrates but also small mammals, other reptiles, birds and their eggs.

Length: HBT 250 cm / 8 ft

Recognition: usually dark-grey or olive-green with conspicuous yellow stripes and markings, and a heavily banded tail.

Habits: spends much of the day patrolling for food and runs quickly when threatened.

Where to find: common near water but also found up trees in wooded savanna and in open grassland.

Feeds on: pretty much anything it can catch, including fish, mammals and birds. It has a taste for crocodile and birds' eggs and will readily scavenge at a carcass and root through lodge waste tips.

Leopard Tortoise *Geochelone pardalis*

Swa: **Kobe**   Maa: **Oloikuma**

Length: HBT 70 cm / 28"

Recognition: the tall, domed shell, or carapace, has a well-marked black-and-gold pattern.

Habits: walks slowly in search of its next meal during all but the hottest parts of the day.

Where to find: open and wooded savanna.

Feeds on: a strictly vegetarian diet, mostly grass and thistles.

This is the largest tortoise in Africa and the fourth largest in the world, with the most impressive specimens weighing in at 40 kg / 88 lbs. They are long-lived animals that can reach 100 years old or more in the right conditions. They can retract their armoured head and legs into their shell so have few predators, but Lions will occasionally use them as playthings before tiring and letting them go.

Tortoises can move remarkably fast when they choose to and can manoeuvre well over rocky ground. Each shell pattern is as unique as a fingerprint.

The male Leopard Tortoise is an aggressive and boisterous lover, grunting noisily and ramming the female's shell to court her, often accompanied by several rival males climbing over the same female. She lays an average of 10 eggs in a hole and these take up to year to hatch.

What's in a name? The scientific name *pardalis* is the same as the Leopard, meaning panther, on account of the distinctive shell pattern.

Top tip: avoid touching or picking up a tortoise as some are known to carry *Salmonella* bacteria.

Helmeted Terrapin *Pelomedusa subrufa*

Swa: **Kasa** Maa: **Oloikuma lankare**

Length: HBT 30 cm / 12"

Recognition: has a flatter, more plain-coloured shell than the Leopard Tortoise, often being matt black or brown. The yellowish head and legs are also longer.

Habits: often seen basking on rocks or branches before dropping into water when disturbed. They wander widely, often crossing tracks, in search of new pools, especially during the rains.

Where to find: seasonally common in marshes and small pools but rarely in large rivers.

Feeds on: almost anything it can catch including tadpoles, worms and crustaceans but also carrion and plant matter.

Also known as the Marsh Terrapin, legend has it that this reptile literally 'fell from the sky' with the first rains! In actual fact, it simply buries itself in the mud when water becomes scarce, a behaviour known as aestivation. This strategy enables the Terrapin to avoid high temperatures and the risk of drying out by entering a dormant state with a reduced metabolic rate.

Male terrapins can be identified by their longer, thicker, pointed tails and are sometimes seen courting females with a nodding head action. Up to 30 eggs are buried by the female and these hatch around three months later.

Flap-necked Chameleon *Chamaeleo dilepis*

Swa: **Kinyonga** Maa: **Tanki**

Length: HBT 43 cm / 17"

Recognition: a chunky, hunch-backed lizard of variable colouration with swivelling eye-sockets and a long and curly prehensile tail.

Habits: typically hides in vegetation but may be found crossing tracks.

Where to find: trees and bushes in woodland, scrub and gardens.

Feeds on: invertebrates, mostly flies.

Chameleons are famous for their remarkable ability to change colour. Their colour changes are primarily linked to emotion (e.g. fear, aggression, social signalling) via the nervous system, rather than camouflage. A message from the brain enlarges or shrinks special chromatophore cells under the top layer of clear skin, causing them to flush with colour pigments. This is similar to a human blushing.

A chameleon's eyes are set within rotating turrets, formed by fused eyelids, and are unique in having the ability to move and focus independently of each other simultaneously. This affords the animal 180-degree vision on each side. Once prey has been located, both eyes focus on the same spot giving the animal a stereoscopic view and acute depth perception.

The chameleon fires its long tongue, armed with a sticky tip, at full speed which scientists have clocked at 1/30th of a second. The insect is pulled into the mouth where it is immediately crushed and eaten. Although this happens far too quickly for the human eye to record, it sometimes makes an audible "*thwack*" on a leaf. The tong-like toes are fused in groups of two and three, and are equipped with sharp claws for climbing. This particular arrangement of toes, known as zygodactylic, is designed for clasping and is also common to parrots and woodpeckers – which, like the chameleon, are able to climb through foliage and up trunks.

What's in a name?
The scientific name derives from the Ancient Greek *chamae leo*, meaning 'dwarf Lion', on account of its aggressive behaviour when threatened

Striped Skink *Mabuya striata*

Swa: **Kasa** Maa: **Empur sambu**

Length: HBT 25 cm / 10"

Recognition: an attractive brown lizard with two cream stripes down the back.

Habits: basks on fallen trees and logs.

Where to find: wooded savanna and in the gardens of lodges and camps with fallen trees or rocks.

Feeds on: invertebrates such as grasshoppers and crickets.

In contrast to the dramatic agama lizards (*page 140*), the skink is a slow and sedate reptile. It seeks food cautiously and with a stuttered motion, shoving its snout in the leaf-litter then pausing and awaiting the movement of a meal. Like the gecko species (*page 138*), the Striped Skink can shed its tail when grasped by a predator, and stump-tailed skinks are a common sight. These skinks are ovoviviparous, hatching their eggs internally and giving birth to live young.

Top tip: despite their amazing camouflage, chameleons can easily be found at night when their skin glows in torchlight.

Length: HBT 15 cm / 6"	
Recognition: a noisy, bug-eyed lizard with rubbery skin.	
Habits: nocturnal, chases bugs around lights at night.	
Where to find: established buildings with electrical lighting.	
Feeds on: small to large invertebrates and other geckos.	

These nocturnal geckos are especially noisy and produce various "clicks" and "chirps" throughout the night as they socialise with other geckos. They are highly variable in colour and pattern. Their vertically-slit pupils are perfectly adapted for night-vision. Like most other gecko species, the Tropical House Gecko lays two soft eggs in crevices. The eggs harden quickly and are protected by the female.

Gecko Gadgets

They may be small and unobtrusive but geckos exhibit some amazing adaptations:

* The ability to run vertically, even upside-down, on smooth surfaces like glass, thanks to specialized toe pads on their webbed feet. Uniquely, this does not involve surface tension (as it does with small insects) but microscopic setae on the toe pads that apply attractive forces to the object on which they are walking.
* A quick-release tail that enables them to escape from predators, a function known as autotomy (see *opposite*).
* A lack of eyelids and the ability to clean their clear eye membranes by licking them with their long tongue.
* Parthenogenic females in some species, meaning they are capable of reproducing without copulating with a male.

Top tip: welcome these harmless lizards into your room as they will kill any bugs including mosquitoes.

Cape Dwarf Gecko *Lygodactylus capensis* Swa: **Mjusi ndogo** Maa: **Empur**

Length: HBT 9 cm / 3½"

Recognition: a tiny lizard with round pupils and camouflaged colouration.

Habits: a daytime hunter of ants and small bugs; usually lives in trees but is adapting to tents.

Where to find: common in and around camps and lodges.

Feeds on: small invertebrates.

The Cape Dwarf Gecko is smaller, slimmer and less noisy than Tropical House Gecko. Although they have adapted to tent poles and canvas, their natural habitat is mature forest, where small colonies are dominated by a single male, which shows a black throat. Approximately 60 species of dwarf gecko have been described, the vast majority from Africa, but more probably await discovery.

Autotomy This Cape Dwarf Gecko has successfully escaped predation by employing caudal autotomy (or 'tail self-severing', from the Latin *caudum* = tail and the Greek *auto* = self + *tomy* = severing). When under attack geckos, skinks and other lizards can shed their tail, which will wriggle and distract the predator while the animal escapes. The tail will partially regenerate (with cartilage replacing the original bone) over a period of a few weeks. Re-grown tails are often a different colour from the rest of the body.

139

Agama drama

Both *Agama* species are medium-sized, long-tailed lizards that change colour according to their mood. Unlike a chameleon, which shows a range of colour variations, the agama is restricted to two combinations: bright and dull. Males are polygamous (*i.e.* they prefer more than one breeding partner, usually five or more) and highly territorial, resulting in great competition for females. Fighting often breaks out between competing males who will try to intimidate opponents with dramatic moves and open mouths. Once the 'boss' has been decided, he will court his delicate females with impressive head bobs and swings (think 'school disco'!). A female in the company of a shy male will wave her rear in front of him before running away until he catches up.

☐ Mwanza Flat-headed Agama
Agama mwanzae

Swa: **Mjusi kafiri**   Maa: **Olmokua oldo lukunya**

Length: HBT 32 cm / 12½"

Recognition: when displaying, males have a pink-red head, neck and back with a blue lower back and tail, turning mostly greyish-blue when relaxed. Females are predominantly brown with a pale neck and scattered white thorny scales.

Habits: basks on rocks to regulate body heat and to display, preferring to run under rocks when threatened.

Where to find: rocky outcrops and pathways, often close to water.

Feeds on: mostly ants, termites and other invertebrates, rarely small amphibians.

Top tip: be patient when trying to photograph lizards. If they run down a lair or up a tree, just sit comfortably nearby and wait for them to start showing off or feasting on the next passing ant swarm.

Male

Female

Blue-headed Tree Agama
Acanthocercus atricollis

Swa: **Mjusi kafiri**
Maa: **Olmokua pus lukunya**

Length: HBT 37 cm / 14½"

Recognition: when displaying, males are recognised by their vivid blue head, turning browner when relaxed, with an obvious pale stripe down the back. Females have obvious black patches on the collar.

Habits: basks on open ground to regulate body heat, running up trees or under bushes or rocks when threatened.

Where to find: open acacia country and short grass plains where it is particularly fond of termite mounds, but also wooded savanna with clearings.

Feeds on: mostly ants, termites and other invertebrates, possibly small amphibians.

At least 37 species of *Agama* have been identified across Africa and many are similar in their behaviour and diet.

Male

Blue-headed Tree Agama
The loss of trees in the Mara, mostly for firewood collection, is a great threat to these colourful reptiles. Although they nest on the ground, they spend most of their day in trees, especially *Bossia* and *Styfolia* species that are found in the dry acacia zone. They are incredibly cautious and run very fast to a bolt hole when threatened. 　　　　*Jackson Looseyia*

☐ Black-necked Spitting Cobra *Naja nigricollis*   Swa: **Swilla**   Maa: **Olasurai Orok**

Length: HBT 2·7 m / 9 ft

Recognition: a slender black or dark-grey snake with wide bars of black and pink on the neck.

Habits: active day and night but most often encountered in the early morning.

Where to find: open and wooded savanna with plentiful termite mounds.

Feeds on: a wide variety of small mammals, reptiles and amphibians.

Although famed for its 'spitting' ability, this dangerous cobra doesn't actually 'spit' venom but 'shoots' it through tiny holes in the fangs. It is able to do so with exceptional accuracy within a 3 m / 10 ft range, usually aiming at the eyes of a threat or predator. It must be stressed that this is not a hunting technique but purely a defence mechanism, causing permanent blindness to untreated eyes; the venom is harmless on the skin. An attack is preceded by a threat display in which the snake inflates its neck into a hood by expanding its neck muscles. It also often raises its head up to 1 m / 3 ft off the ground for greater intimidating effect. However, the most dangerous cobra is one that bites, for this snake kills its prey with a potent cytotoxin that quickly breaks down the cells of its prey's organs and body tissue, causing a slow and painful death.

It is believed in Maasai culture that if a Spitting Cobra visits a young or pregnant woman in her home, her first born will be a boy. ***Joseph Ole Kima***

Like most other tribes in East Africa, the Maasai people do not like snakes but when a Spitting Cobra enters our home, we should never kill them. Our tradition says that it should be left a bowl of milk, preferably next to firewood where the snake will feel safe. Although a snake has never been observed drinking the milk, it is the action that appeases them and they will leave you and your family in peace. Also, should a Spitting Cobra cross your path you will receive good luck in the future. ***David Lekada Mpusia***

Black Mamba *Dendroaspis polylepis*

Swa: **Koboko** Maa: **Olasurai Ngioro**

Length: HBT 4 m / 13 ft

Recognition: a slender snake, usually olive grey-brown in colouration with paler underparts. The pale coffin-shaped head contrasts with black beady eyes.

Habits: diurnal, usually located in trees but will sometimes travel along the ground.

Where to find: savanna and woodland, where it is fond of trees, termite mounds and other sites with protective bolt-holes.

Feeds on: a variety of mammals, birds and other reptiles, including snakes.

The Black Mamba gets its name from the ink-black colouration of the inside of the mouth and not its skin colour. Reaching lengths in excess of 4 m / 13 ft, this formidable predator is the longest venomous snake in Africa. It is very fast on the ground, often travelling on the rear half of the body alone, and is claimed by many to be the world's fastest snake, able to reach speeds of 20 kph / 12 mph. The Black Mamba has a reputation for attacking humans without provocation. Such attacks often involve female snakes protecting their eggs, and no mamba should be approached without an expert present. The fast-acting venom contains a deadly mix of neurotoxins which affect the brain, and cardiotoxins which affect the heart and muscle tissue. Rarely, you may encounter two snakes writhing together in combat which could be mistaken for mating behaviour.

It's not only people that are scared of this snake – many birds are too. Most birds, including starlings and sunbirds, have a 'dangerous snake' alarm call which can be really useful when trying to find snakes – or avoid them! ***Petro Naurori***

Length: HBT 1·2 m / 4 ft
Recognition: a slender, heavily-marked snake with large-eyes and a pointed snout.
Habits: diurnal, very fast and incredibly agile.
Where to find: wooded savanna, riverine woodland and forest.
Feeds on: small reptiles including dwarf geckos and lizards.

☐ Spotted Bush Snake
Philothamnus semivariegatus

Swa: **Nyoka ukuti** Maa: **Olasurai onyori**

The Spotted Bush Snake is rarely seen on the ground as it prefers to hunt in trees and bushes. It is heavily scaled underneath which gives it excellent traction and it has been known to climb smooth tree trunks that appear to offer it no grip at all. Of all the snakes the authors have encountered in East Africa, this one has the habit of turning up in the unlikeliest of places, including vehicle dashboards and dining rooms!

☐ Velvety-green Night Adder
Causus resimus

Swa: **Nyoka kijani** Maa: **Olasurai onyori**

Length: HBT 70 cm / 28"
Recognition: a small but well-proportioned leaf-green snake with velvety-skin and small black flecks down the spine and flanks.
Habits: despite the name, it is active day and night but can be difficult to find in its woodland habitat.
Where to find: wooded savanna and riverine woodland.
Feeds on: mostly toads and frogs but also small invertebrates.

This attractive terrestrial snake may be encountered on trails and pathways through well-wooded areas. Bites from this snake are rarely recorded because it has adopted an impressive display to warn off threats. This involves inflating itself and hissing loudly, which is usually enough to draw attention and avoid people accidentally standing on it.

Puff Adder *Bitis arietans*

Length: HBT 1·9 m / 6 ft

Recognition: a fat-bodied and highly camouflaged snake, with a broad, triangular head.

Habits: sluggish, terrestrial and mostly nocturnal, when it lies in ambush or searches small holes for prey.

Where to find: open and wooded savanna, acacia scrub and forest edge.

Feeds on: mostly rodents and other small vertebrates.

The statistics speak for themselves: more people die in Africa from a Puff Adder bite than from any other snake. However, unlike the Black Mamba (*page 143*), they are not an overtly aggressive snake and most attacks occur because victims stand on them accidentally. This happens for three reasons: they are incredibly well-camouflaged; they are reluctant to move when in danger; and they are mostly active at night when people tend to look ahead rather than at the ground. Like the Spitting Cobra (*page 142*), the venom is cytotoxic, causing similar cell malfunction. Unlike many other snakes, the Puff Adder moves in a straight line, caterpillar-fashion, rather than with a writhing motion.

African Rock Python *Python natalensis*

Length: HBT 6 m / 20 ft

Recognition: a long, thick-bodied snake with a broad, spear-like head. The greyish, leathery skin is covered with brown and rusty patches of various sizes.

Habits: prefers to hunt at night but is often seen basking in the morning sun.

Where to find: this nomadic species could be encountered in any habitat.

Feeds on: mammals up to the size of gazelle and, less frequently, birds and reptiles.

This is the largest snake in Africa and although the record length in Kenya measured 6 m / 20 ft, specimens up to 9·8 m / 32 ft long have been claimed in the central African forests! African Rock Python has very rarely been known to kill and eat humans. It locates its warm-blooded prey with heat-seeking pits on the snout and strikes with a fearsome mouth full of very sharp teeth. Once caught, the prey is immediately smothered by the coiling body of the snake and slowly crushed with an intensifying grip. Experts have suggested that the prey actually dies from a heart attack rather than suffocation. Pythons are able to unhinge their jaws to facilitate swallowing large animals but this process can take many hours. Once inside the snake, prey can take many weeks, even months, to be digested and such well-fed beasts do not need to eat very often. Unusually among snakes, female pythons are fantastic mothers, guarding their eggs (up to 100 although 30 is more common) with vigilance, and later the hatchlings, for several weeks. It is thought that pythons are one of most primitive of all snake families as their skeletons possess vestigal limbs, suggesting they have not changed much from their earlier 'lizard days'.

When I was young a friend and I were led by a wonderful bird called a honeyguide to an olive tree that was laden with fruit and, apparently, honey. As my friend climbed high to reach the beehive, I suddenly noticed that the 'hive' had a moving tail and was in fact a very large, coiled-up Rock Python that was ready to strike at him. My friend was very lucky and avoided a strike – but only then did I understand why the honeyguide wanted our help so much.

Joseph Ole Kima

References and useful resources

References

The Kingdon Field Guide to African Mammals by Jonathan Kingdon

A Field Guide to the Reptiles of East Africa by Stephen Spawls, Kim Howell, Robert Drewes and James Ashe

The Safari Companion: A Guide to Watching African Mammals by Richard D. Estes

Online resources

www.maasaimara.com
For unbiased, informative, accurate and up to date information on all things relating to the Masai Mara National Reserve. The expert team also produces a must-have tourist guide book which is available at most camps and lodges in and around the reserve.

www.naturekenya.org
The very friendly and professional team is always there to assist in any matter relating to the wildlife of Kenya and I highly recommend joining the organisation.

www.elephantsandbees.com
This amazing project explores the use of African Honey Bees as a deterrent to African Elephants, thus reducing crop damage and conflict with people. Dr Lucy King and her team would really appreciate your support – so please log on and see what the buzz is all about!

www.lionconservation.org/mara-predator-project.html
Check out the Mara Predator Project, operated by Living With Lions, the conservation research organisation that is battling to save Africa's remaining Lions. If you have quality high-resolution images of wild Lions, these could be really useful to the team – so log on to see how you can get involved.

www.tusk.org
Get involved with the organisation that is "Protecting Wildlife, Supporting Communities, Promoting Education" in Africa.

Acknowledgements

We are very grateful for the encouragement to produce this photographic guide from many friends and colleagues that we have met on the East African safari circuit over the years. But one group stands out above all others in terms of their enthusiasm for this project – the guides of the Masai Mara.

In particular, we must offer heartfelt thanks to the guides of Naibor Camp, past and present, who fuelled our passion for this spectacular corner of the world. They have each expanded our knowledge of the animals of the Mara immensely, and for that we shall always be grateful. We would particularly like to thank Nelson Kirrokorr, David Mpusia, Mathew Lalaigwanani, Nkalma "Lolo" Lolotuno, Ledukan "Daudi" Lolotuno, David Mpoe, Petro Naurori, Daniel Naurori and Dennis Muli. Keep up the amazing work guys and continue to be great ambassadors for your people, both Maasai and Samburu, and guardians of the wildlife that you cherish so dearly. But most of all, keep smiling!

We are especially thankful to our 'Fabulous Four' guides who so generously shared their knowledge and experiences with us, and whose contributions greatly enrich this book. Thanks also to Topioka "John" Pesi for his assistance with the naming of species in the Maa language. Ashe oleng!

For their friendship and unwavering support at all times, thanks go to our Mara neighbours, Jono Raynor and Dudu Beaton. For their warm hospitality and all-round brilliance, we would also like to thank the following: Philip and Kate McLellan and the awesome team at Governors' Camp, Magdelle Dempers and all staff at &Beyond's Kichwa Tembo / Bateleur Camps (we love you guys!), and the friendly team at Siana Springs. A special mention also to the team at Asilia for their kindness and support during our numerous visits to Naboisho and Rekero Camps.

Our venture into Africa would never have been possible without the Fox family, especially Bruce and Jane who were brave enough to take a chance on us to manage their camps in Tanzania even though we had no prior experience. The heads of the family, Geoff and Vicky Fox, were especially kind and helpful to us and we shall always be grateful to them for the opportunities they have given us.

Finally, to the team at **WILD**Guides: Rob Still, Andy and Gill Swash, and Brian Clews (designer, editors and proof-reader extraordinaire) – you have once again weaved your magic to help us create something quite beautiful. We shall always be grateful for your hard work and diligence in bringing our dreams to life. Thank you.

Photographic credits

All images included in this book were taken by the authors, Adam Scott Kennedy and Vicki Kennedy, with the exception of the following:

Small-spotted Genet (*p. 42*); Slender Mongoose (*p. 50*); Aardvark (*p. 61*); Striped Ground Squirrel (*p. 111*); Crested Porcupine (*p. 113*): **Greg & Yvonne Dean / WorldWildlifeImages.com**.

Wild Cat (*p. 40*): **Peter Bagnall / PeterBagnall-photography.co.uk**.

Zorilla (*p. 54*): **Ian Beames / Ardea.com**.

Pangolin (*p. 60*): **Angus Hart / flickr.com/photos/angushart**.

Mountain Reedbuck (*p. 92*).

Index

This index includes the common English and *scientific* names of all the mammals and reptiles included in this book.

Common names in **bold** highlight the species that are afforded a full account.

Bold numbers indicate the page number of the main species account.

Blue numbers relate to other page(s) on which a photograph appears.

Normal black numbers are used to indicate the page(s) where other species are mentioned, but not illustrated.